THE QUAKER APPROACH

The Quaker Approach

To Contemporary Problems

EDITED BY JOHN KAVANAUGH
Public Relations Director
American Friends Service Committee

George Allen & Unwin Ltd
RUSKIN HOUSE · MUSEUM STREET · LONDON

FIRST PUBLISHED IN 1953
Copyright in U.S.A.

This book is copyright under the Berne Convention. Apart from any fair dealing for the purposes of private study, research, criticism or review, as permitted under the Copyright Act 1911, no portion may be reproduced by any process without written permission. Enquiry should be made to the publisher.

PRINTED IN GREAT BRITAIN BY
BISHOP AND SONS LTD.
EDINBURGH

Preface

THE INCENTIVE for this book was the result of the many inquiries which have come to the American Friends Service Committee in the last few years for information regarding the "Quaker point of view" on social, economic, and political problems. The book, therefore, attempts to show how the principles of the Religious Society of Friends are applicable to contemporary human affairs by showing how they have been applied by Friends to specific problems over the years.

While there has never been common agreement among Friends as to the best remedies for the problems that beset the world, the "urge of social concern" has always been present in the Society, for Friends believe that religion and life are inseparable. For three hundred years this urge has impelled many Friends to seek earnestly and continuously to bring light to bear on the major issues of their day.

It is true that the dedicated social pioneering of a relatively few has given the Society of Friends a reputation far beyond any that it deserves; and that the favorable position which it enjoys today is due largely to the accomplishments of early Friends. Nevertheless, the Quaker approach is as valid today as it was earlier, and the same opportunities for social pioneering —in far greater number—are open to all concerned persons, Quakers and others alike.

It is hoped, therefore, that this book will be helpful, not only in interpreting the Quaker approach to human problems, but also in inspiring to thought and action those seekers who would like to dedicate their lives to human progress.

The editor wishes to express his appreciation to the authors, all members of the Society of Friends, who agreed, in spite of busy schedules and short notices, to contribute papers; also to Sally Longstreth for her aid in reading and editing the manuscripts, and to the girls in the American Friends Service Committee offices who did the typing.

Appreciation is extended likewise to Guilford College for permission to use the paper written by Howard Brinton and originally given as the *Second Ward Lecture*.

Lastly it should be stated that although an effort was made to co-ordinate the material, the autonomous nature of each chapter made a certain amount of overlapping desirable. Also, the editor assumes full responsibility for the book in its final form since the papers were not resubmitted to the authors.

John Kavanaugh

Contents

Preface		v
Introduction	Janet Whitney	ix
1. Peace and War	Henry J. Cadbury	3
2. Relief and Reconstruction	Roger C. Wilson	25
3. Economic Life	Kenneth E. Boulding	43
4. Business and Industry	D. Robert Yarnall	61
5. Education	Howard H. Brinton	73
6. Race Relations	Ira De A. Reid	91
7. Civil Liberties	Harrop A. Freeman	115
8. Crime and Punishment	Curtis Bok	137
9. Prisons and Prisoners	Henry Van Etten	143
10. Science	Kathleen Lonsdale	163
11. Health and Healing	Howard E. Collier	183
12. Present Secular Philosophies	D. Elton Trueblood	203
13. Quakers and the Russians	Elmore Jackson	221
Epilogue	Clarence E. Pickett	241

Introduction

BY

JANET WHITNEY

Author of four biographies: *John Woolman—American Quaker, Elizabeth Fry, Abigail Adams,* and *Geraldine Cadbury.* Novels: *Jennifer, Judith,* and *Intrigue in Baltimore.*

IN PRESENTING such a book as this to the general public it is by no means the Quaker intention to seem to be saying "God I thank thee that I am not as other men are." But what the Religious Society of Friends stands for has to be constantly re-expressed and offered to the world in concrete illustration as well as in precept, because it is essentially, as the title here says, an approach and not a platform.

The Society of Friends is not a relief Society, nor a peace Society, but its activities along both these lines are so well known, of such long standing, that they have become distinctive in the public mind. The American Friends Service Committee in the United States and the Friends Service Council in England are their most modern expression.

The fight of the early Quakers to obtain freedom for their peculiar religious practices and their resistance to military service in time of war has made them pioneers and experts in the cause of civil liberty.

The imprisonment of their own members in the first generation of Quakers called their attention early to the treatment of prisoners. George Fox in prison was as much concerned over the neglected rights of criminals awaiting trial, and as eager to plead their cause before the justices, as he was about his co-religionists who were in prison for conscience' sake.

George Fox was himself gifted as a hypnotic healer of the sick; and the profession of medicine, which in the early days did not require a University training, was one of the few learned professions open to Quakers, therefore one which they were liable to enter. For different reasons the latter holds true today.

Quaker schools took a high place in the educational world from the beginning, both for the thoroughness and all-roundedness of their training, and from the fact that girls were given an equal education with boys before that idea became generally accepted. George Fox's liberal foundation principle was that both boys and girls should be taught "all things useful to the creation." Fox himself did not happen to consider music or the arts or secular literature "useful to the creation." But he left no dead hand to restrain their introduction. These subjects are no longer considered "frivolities" in a Quaker school curriculum but are seen as openings for the spirit.

In business, Quakers, as a necessary result of their yea and nay practice in private and civil life, were the first to introduce the one-price system. They do not, however, claim on account of this that their integrity is greater than the integrity of other honest businessmen. The modern idea of service as a basis of successful business, and the efficient salesmanship which establishes friendly relations with customer or client, were known and practiced, as a result of his natural love for his fellow man, by John Woolman, the Quaker pre-Revolution apostle of simplicity, and brought the inevitable business success. John Woolman did not want business success (in the form, at least, of wealth) for reasons of his own, and withdrew from it, finally having to give up his business entirely in order to avoid it. But not all Quakers share his point of view. Every Quaker confronted by wealth obtained through legitimate activity has to deal with his own problem for himself.

Quakers also have varying opinions as to how to apply their

principles in the field of politics. But they are all one in the root principle of the eternal value of the individual—"that of God in every man." This carries the logical sequence of universal brotherhood and liberty of conscience. Quakers cannot become members of secret societies, because such societies by their very nature narrow this unity and deny this liberty. For the same reason Quakers cannot link themselves with any totalitarian movement such as Nazism, Fascism or Communism.

That brings us to another reason for the presentation of this book. Quakers have no set of rules, no synod or governing body, no Bishop or Pope or President. Each Yearly Meeting is a self-governing unit, well organized within itself on a general Quaker pattern, but actually accountable to no other. What holds the world-wide Society of Friends together was exemplified in the World Conference at Oxford, England, in the summer of 1952, when 900 delegates met from Friends Yearly Meetings all over the world. The bond is partly historical, their reference to their common origin; and partly the system of Queries and Advices, regularly read in the local Monthly Meetings, and (though not identical in all the various Books of Discipline) derived from the original Queries and Advices of George Fox's time. These piercing questions and pithy counsels keep Quakers everywhere approximating to a certain common standard of belief, theory, and practice, while laying no rigid bonds of the letter on the freedom of the spirit.

Since the life and thought of such a Society is always on the move, following the Light, and has nothing to hold it back from new experiment and adventure in God's will but the natural conservatism of the human heart, books like this one serve to report from time to time where we have got to. By choosing certain representative individuals, experts in their particular fields, to give us the gist of their experience, we can check up with ourselves, and communicate to our neighbors, what Quakers are now about. We offer the result humbly, in a spirit of sharing with our fellow human beings who like us are trying to find the meaning of life on this earth.

September, 1952

Peace and War
BY
HENRY J. CADBURY

I

Peace and War

BY

HENRY J. CADBURY

Hollis Professor of Divinity, Harvard University; Chairman, Executive Board, American Friends Service Committee; author of many books in the field of Religion.

THERE IS NOTHING unique nowadays in praising peace. Few persons, even in the military profession, any longer regard war as desirable or glorious. Nearly everyone professes to prefer peace, and the protestations of individuals and nations are mainly sincere. The differences are in areas other than the universal approbation of peace. By what methods does one expect to preserve or secure peace? Is peace preferable to conditions which one hopes by war to prevent or to remove? Can one have one's way in certain circumstances without war? Or is the price of peace higher than one is willing to pay? Thomas à Kempis said, "All men desire peace, but not all men will do that which belongeth to peace." Many of the above questions involve disputable factors, and undoubtedly many subjective differences accompany the varying answers to these questions. There is naturally difference of opinion as to the effectiveness of war, the moral justification of war, the available alternatives to war.

The Quaker approach to peace is subject to all these causes for variation. If I were to pick out two characteristic features of the relation of the Society of Friends to war, I think one would be their emphasis upon the problem as a religious, or in other terms, a moral, a spiritual, or a psychological problem. The other would be their seemingly negative emphasis on personal abstention. In connection with these the whole character of "the Quaker peace testimony," as it is often called, can be most easily understood.

At the outset one must indicate that this testimony is not to be defined in the authoritative terms of either a full-fledged philosophy or an elaborated technique. A singularly unregimented group of individualists over a period of three centuries, with a strong aversion to codification of either belief or practice, does not offer an easy task to the portrait painter. What can be described is a prevailing trend, an unconscious pattern, a recurrent set of phenomena, nonetheless consistent for not having the kinds of controls that logic or ecclesiastical direction often supplies. Both in its motivation and in its rationale the Friends' position will appear naïve. Insofar as it is articulate it will seem to many oversimplified, though on reflection one must confess that the alternative or opposite positions are often oversimplified if one takes into account the complexity of inner personal life and of the society with which we have to deal.

The negative side of the Quaker position would be called today religious pacifism or conscientious objection. Taking quite literally the Biblical commands "Thou shalt not kill" and "Love your enemies" and "Overcome evil with good," the early Friends applied them to war and to personal participation in war. Much else in the New Testament and even in the Old confirmed their attitude. Few of them knew as well as we know today of later Christian espousal of the same position; that the writings of the Church before Constantine indicate that Christians generally for three hundred years avoided military action either for or against the state. Nearer their own time, as early Friends may sporadically have known, in England and on the Continent, small groups of Christian extremists in theory and in practice rejected military service. The more conventional Christians in their writings noted among heretical views of the sects the view that it was unlawful to bear arms for the state. Influenced by these forerunners, though unaware of them, the Friends came to the same position, often independently of one another, and gradually.

George Fox, the first Quaker, in 1650 declined a captaincy in the army; by 1661, he and others stated as the official position of the group their abjuring all use of outward weapons. Friends in the army in the meantime withdrew, unless indeed they were first discharged by the military on other grounds. The position since that time has been many times reaffirmed officially, as in 1684, in 1775, in 1914–19. Individual Friends have occasionally rejected the position or restricted it to "aggressive" wars. They are not in the stream of Quaker tendencies. Popular and governmental recognition has long shown its acceptance of this equivalence of Quaker and pacifist. In the eighteenth century, wooden dummy cannon carried by merchant ships to discourage pirate capture were nicknamed "Quaker guns." At times and places where conscriptive legislation or regulations have made exceptions for conscience it was expected that Quakers would fall under the ruling. Military-minded patriots if well informed have always had the consolation of knowing that the Quaker will not fight for the other side either, though more often in a partisan situation his refusal has been construed as allegiance to the other side, as personal selfishness, or as indifference to the good cause.

For the Friend himself the position is quite different. He gives the problem of partisanship little thought. He is impelled by a feeling of the wrongness of war in general. To refuse to take part in it seems a natural corollary. Indeed in most areas of his environment the general standard of theory is personal nonparticipation in evil practices, whether they are individual or collective. When, for example, the churches with great unanimity declare that "War is contrary to the will of God," the next sentence would naturally begin with the word *therefore* rather than with *but*. "Therefore a Christian may not take part in war." To the Quaker it seems strange that most Christians of other churches draw no such conclusion.

From this beginning the next question is not what effect will war refusal have on me, nor what effect will conduct like mine have on the general situation, but what must I do to take no part in war. For very soon it becomes evident that at least in our society the business of war enters into much of our whole civilian economy. This question is more insistent than the other questions, because while they are questions addressed to the future, there is often an immediate issue. "Where do I draw the line?" Is it against combatant service only? against noncombatant service in uniform? against alternative service performed under more or less military supervision or control, or at least under the terms of legislation intended in the main to prepare for or to prosecute a war? The experience in the Society of Friends is that such questions have to be faced when they arise by the individual conscience, that the conscience may become increasingly sensitive with time, and that neither uniformity nor convincing logic can be expected. The sensitizing of conscience means that what to one generation or one period of an individual's life seems inoffensive may later be condemned.

This progressive extension of conscience can be illustrated in other areas of conduct or in other groups. For Friends and war it has been repeated again and again. Men who without qualm or scruple have accepted military service have for themselves come "to see to the end of wars and fighting," and have been compelled to clear their conscience of further complicity step by step. The logic of further steps was not always evident. In 1666 some Quaker carpenters at shipyards on the Thames felt forced to quit when their employers, for fear of raids from the hostile Dutch, required them to carry arms while at their work. That the ships they were building were to be ships of war does not seem to have bothered them. Nor apparently did it bother William Penn, usually a model pacifist, to endorse in 1709 a petition to the Treasury on behalf of several merchants (also probably Quakers) proposing "to furnish her Majesty's ships of war in the West Indies, Maryland and Virginia with provisions from Pennsylvania in America at cheaper rates, fresher and better than usually sent from England and other parts of Europe."

One would suppose that consistent Friends would recognize

that the manufacture of guns and cannon was wrong. There have been those who did not, while other Quaker industries have continuously refused to sell even civilian types of goods through the military requisitions of government. Taxes for war purposes have again and again raised problems for Friends, with no final solution of universal approval or disapproval. To mention only two not well-known cases, Francis Daniel Pastorius two centuries and a half ago argued that if included in a general taxation budget they might be paid, while Job Scott in 1780 took the opposite view. Each of these Friends wrote a pamphlet on the subject but neither was ever published, having failed at the time to secure official approval. In modern times some Friends have refused to pay at least that proportion of income tax which corresponds to the proportion of the national budget spent on military matters. That the government has ways of collecting these amounts without consent has doubtless discouraged others from attempting refusal.

In the case of more direct conscription for military service, young men have more difficult decisions to make. In different times and places the issue has presented itself quite differently. It is natural, however, that the Quaker conscience should extend its refusal sometimes to military training quite as much as to military service, to ambulance work, hospital service, or even civilian relief when controlled, prescribed, or permitted by the military, or to registration under a conscription act.

Guard duties have raised other questions on which unanimity among pacifists is not to be expected. "Watching" without weapons was approved by some Friends in the seventeenth century and disapproved by others. Civilian defense, whether voluntary or compulsory, has been refused by some Friends in modern times, particularly when it has appeared to be more intended to establish a war psychology than to reduce the loss of life.

The perplexity caused by such questions is real, but it should not be exaggerated. Nor should a group in general agreement be disturbed by difference of personal judgment. There are some persons no doubt who, because they find no easy way to avoid complicity in war, or no convincing logical ground for drawing the line at a given point, abandon the attempt at personal nonparticipation. They can argue that since I cannot be consistently good, why not be inconsistently bad? Their real reasons are probably different. The pressure of public opinion, especially in time of actual war, the desire for solidarity with others, the arguments and atmosphere strongly sanctioning war, and the personal disadvantage involved in noncompliance, all tend to reinforce this inner difficulty. The terms *consistent* and *absolute* are taken seriously by such a person, whereas it is little realized how the unabashed warrior also draws arbitrary lines and so violates both adjectives.

The essence of the Quaker position is its inner noncompliance with war, and this goes much more deeply than the issues of personal involvement. It does not absolve one from courageous dissent at places where the state compels decision, but in democratic countries conscientious dissent has a much wider range of responsibility. Here again only individual judgment can be relied upon to dictate courses of conduct and action. It may lead to individual or collective protest, and to individual and collective action. One may cite the antiwar statesmanship of John Bright, the unbroken collective testimony of Friends officially, and the positive acts and examples to be mentioned hereafter. To keep oneself free inwardly from consent is often a task that requires all one's strength. The unspoken but known dissent of single individuals or small groups often challenges the conscience of those who know and respect them more eloquently than do dramatic deeds or cogent arguments.

The consequences of such an unpopular stand are not pleasant. Experience has taught Friends what they may be. Some migrations of Friends and other pacifist Christians from Europe to this country were to escape the conflict over conscription and military service. Frequently in Britain and her dependencies the mere refusal of Friends to illuminate their houses after military victory precipitated mob violence, while the maltreatment of unwilling conscripts by the military has been frequent even if unauthorized. Along with physical tortures there have been social ostracism, economic discrimination and, perhaps the hardest of all, misunderstanding on the part of many whom one loves and respects. There is no need to describe these sufferings in detail. They have taken different forms in different circumstances. They are the natural result of the strong feelings which patriotism rouses when its conventional demands are refused. The sufferer is usually prepared to expect such results, though others may out of indignation or a sense of injustice seek to secure for him protection by law. Like the good soldier himself, he would rather be loyal to the duty he sees than protect his own comfort. His act is an act of obedience, come what may. As William Penn expressed it, the Quaker's choice is "not fighting, but suffering."

The charges against which the pacifist position must defend itself are legion. Throughout their history Friends have had opportunity to hear them frequently and to reflect upon them. Every generation will hear them in somewhat different terms and will have to deal with them freshly in the light of their contemporary thinking.

Is it not a form of selfishness to set your own conscientious preferences over against the common cause as accepted by your countrymen, who often share your moral distaste for war? Is it not disloyalty to your country to which you owe so much, and whose benefits and protection you accept without responding to its demands? Especially in a democracy or under a union of nations may the will of the majority be lightly set aside by personal whim? Logically, ought you not renounce all other use of force, in the treatment of children, the insane, the criminal? Is not war justified by the analogy of the police? Granted that wars of the past have sometimes been unjustified, this war is different. Are there not greater evils than war? And under the circumstances what else can you do, since some nations are bent on evil and understand no language except force?

These and the other familiar challenges need not be answered here. It is not claimed that Friends have all the answers; they do know most of the questions. If these challenges seem to influence Friends less than they do others, it is not because of a different or better logic. Their tradition helps them see as John Bright once said "that nineteen out of every twenty wars which have been waged ought to have been avoided and were criminal in the highest degree." Their faith in people, even in the enemy, undercuts the usual pessimism about alternative procedures. They are not persuaded that wholesale murder at the command of a democratic government or even of a world government is thereby moralized. The choice of war as the lesser of two evils is, of course, as speculative a judgment as the reverse. Friends admit the risk of not going to war, but even the warrior gambles amid uncertainties. In the long run the advantages of war, even those of apparent immediate self-interest for our nation or group of nations, may be neutralized by the complicated long range results. It was a realist, Georges Clemenceau, not a pacifist, who said, "There are things worse than war but war is the cause of all of them."

A widespread use is made in Quaker thought of the distinction of war as a method from either its "causes" or its objectives. Friends may sympathize with the alleged ends of a war; they may recognize as facts the situation which seems to others to recommend war. But that war is the way to deal with this situation or to strive toward these ends does not automatically follow. If flagrant abuse of its own citizens or of other peoples is practiced by a foreign power, violence on our part may involve other innocent persons and may not reduce the evil results, merely relocate or change them. Friends would challenge the assumption that war is the appropriate answer to recognized evil-doing in others or the obvious means to recognized good goals. The habitual reliance on military strength as a tool or as a threat tends to divert attention from seeking other means for worthy ends. Granted the purest motives for waging war, it is an open question whether the ends justify the means or whether the means (war) will really accomplish those ends. Peace ultimately has to come by persuasion not force, and war often makes more difficult rather than easier the right peaceful settlement which it is hoped that military victory will achieve.

Another common assumption condoning war is that defense by such means is morally justified—defense whether of ourselves, of other persons, or even of ideas and ideals. History does not indicate that war successfully protects the innocent even on one side. Quite apart from doubt whether war does really defend, it is increasingly difficult in most modern circumstances to distinguish defense and aggression. The citizen of every country is now informed that his country is defending itself even if the conflict, as with recent American wars, is thousands of miles from its frontiers. In other cases much depends on obscure data, or technical definition. Military experts now recommend prior action on our part as a method of defense, since strategically much will depend on an initial advantage so gained. Both sides can claim a defensive purpose, as in the American Civil War when the North was defending the Union and the South was defending the rights of States. Once any war is started each side is obviously on the defense. The distinction of aggression and defense is often based on a stop-watch distinction and thereafter the procedures of both sides are equally unrestrained, though each side justifies itself and condemns the other on the ground that from some point in the past it was the attacked and not the attacker. The moral question, rarely raised, is whether the defender is justified. Even nonpacifists deny that we have the right to use any and every means to protect our homes and persons and countries. What the Gospels deal with is not the wrongness of aggression but the duty of the person wronged or attacked not to strike back.

The Quaker's task of maintaining his position against these and other familiar arguments, even to himself, is no easy one. In time of actual war it is particularly difficult, and the difficulty is not confined to young men subject to military service. Others also are exposed to the pressure of conformity to current moods and arguments and do not feel loyal to Quaker tradition if they inwardly acquiesce in the war-making philosophy. Undoubtedly tradition and the solidarity of their Society give them strength, but they are also part of a larger nonpacifist community whose sincerity and assurance cannot be ignored. The very fact of their minority position is a powerful challenge. Their relative idleness in time of war fever compels them to think more deeply than if they simply shared the dominant mood about them. It was an observation true to modern experience which in the famous Song of Deborah (Judges 5:16) assigns only to the nonparticipants in war the "searchings of heart."

Difficult and sometimes all-absorbing as is the abstention in act and thought from consent to war, the conscientious pacifist or Quaker counts this as much less than his whole duty. He is constrained to do more than avoid evil doing. He must "Depart from evil, and do good; Seek peace, and pursue it." The positive requirements of his position are the more weighty as he believes that he is called upon to bear testimony by work and example to the more excellent way. The positive side of the Quaker approach to peace is inseparable from the negative. They supplement each other, are consistent with each other, and neither can be expected to be effective without the other, though in given circumstances one is sometimes better able to present one side more effectively than the other. Without an alternative service of a peacemaking character, his refusal of war-making would seem to himself and others too cheaply bought.

For this reason the Quaker, historically speaking, has been found conspicuously in the ranks of the peacemakers. That has been true since the beginning of the English-speaking peace societies early in the nineteenth century. Collective action or agitation by Friends alone or by Friends in conjunction with others has been the order of the day.

As associates with Friends in this effort, those persons who approach the matter from a Christian angle have naturally proved most congenial. Most recently these religious pacifists, though a relatively small proportion of church membership, have shown their courage in standing out against the sanction of wars given by the prevailing church leadership. Since 1915 the Fellowship of Reconciliation has brought many of them into association with each other and with many Friends. During most of the same period Friends, Mennonites, and the Church of the Brethren—the three best-known pacifist churches—have found fellowship with each other.

Co-operation with other non-Quaker groups is less simple

and poses the Society of Friends a problem. Genuine opposition to war and to specific trends toward war is widespread. How far can a group like the Quakers work effectively with these several groups and on specific campaigns? To refrain on the ground that Friends are more sincere or consistent would be absurd. Yet experience shows that alliances of this kind are sometimes not lasting. Official peace societies have changed so as to condone or encourage war. Some movements of our time are so plainly politically or partisanly oriented as to be fosterers of war—hot or cold. To many Friends in 1951 both the Stockholm Petition and the Crusade for Freedom appeared to be equivalent examples. Organizations on behalf of the League of Nations or the United Nations insofar as they support military sanctions hardly agreed with a Quaker condemnation of all wars. It has always been possible in time of war to persuade certain kinds of peace lovers that this particular war was for securing a permanent peace.

Opposition to war, like alliance for war, produces strange bedfellows. One recalls the time after World War I when an association for the prevention of war, largely supported by Friends, found that the brewers, afraid of the return to America of wartime prohibition, were lending it financial support. There is every reason why nearly every category of citizen— taxpayers, mothers, international exporters, tourist agents, to mention only a few examples—should oppose war for reasons not quite the same as those of Friends. In every war there are some of our fellow citizens who have good reason to sympathize with the "other side."

If he that is not for us is against us, the pacifist seems to be an ally of the enemy. Superficially the religious pacifist resembles many persons of different ilk. He is in danger of being used by them for their own purposes, and confused with them by his prowar neighbors. The Quakers can lose respectability or give respectability by such association and are, therefore, often best satisfied to operate independently of promiscuous and ill-defined parties or movements. At the same time, they recognize that increasingly persons of integrity, without taking the full pacifist position, share the Quaker ideals and motivation in matters connected with world peace. On issues that arise in foreign policy they welcome such alliance and association. They know they have no monopoly on such concerns as increasing reliance on nonmilitary methods of avoiding war. They can, therefore, go a long way in co-operating with efforts toward disarmament, negotiation and arbitration, international neighborliness, and assistance.

In speaking, therefore, of more exclusively Quaker enterprises it is not intended to imply that they are unique in kind. They may be characteristic of Quakerism because they grow out of characteristic Quaker attitudes. The underlying renunciation of war as an alternative colors them, both for the Quaker participant and for the outsider. At the same time they often commend themselves to persons who do not share the underlying renunciation; they challenge them to thought and even to imitation.

Illustrations might be drawn from more remote times or places, but I shall draw mainly upon items within my own experience—in the present century and in American Quakerism. It is my steady contention that quite unconsciously Quakerism conforms to a somewhat consistent expression of its historic position, no matter how different the intellectual climate in which ancient Friends moved.

In attempting to spread their pacifist conviction, Friends have appealed to the mind as well as to the conscience. They are convinced that wars are not inevitable either through God's willing them, or by some kind of impersonal necessity. They can endorse the words in the preamble to the charter of UNESCO: "Since wars are made in the minds of men it is in the minds of men that the defenses of peace must be created." They rule out thus any talk of divine necessity—what the insurance companies call "an act of God," somewhat blasphemously—and they recognize war and peace as lying in the lap of men. While events may move in such a way as to make war probable, men themselves can halt at the brink and should be encouraged to do so, and even when war has begun, early cessation is to be preferred to continued carnage and to the deteriorating conditions under which peace must be made. Unconditional surrender is psychologically deleterious for both victor and vanquished. Even some military experts regard overwhelming victory as politically disadvantageous.

Friends believe that both sides are amenable to reason and that in the tension that precedes, accompanies, or follows war, the appeal to reason must be exercised to the full. Their efforts, which seem to others indiscriminately "in season and out of season," are due to an imperturbable confidence that there is something of God in all men to which they can and must appeal. Apart from their application of their principles to a concrete contemporary situation, they are eager to examine the phenomena of war as objectively as possible and to indicate its irrelevance as method to the supposed causes of war or to its probable result. Their standing disavowal of the process perhaps enables them to look at it more objectively and from a more complete set of perspectives. A typical Institute of International Relations conducted by Friends is not likely to deal exclusively with political, military, or economic considerations but with each of them in turn and then with analysis of values along psychological, sociological, and ethical lines. By cultivating such approaches and by stimulating others to a commitment to the resultant finding, they aim to reduce the war-breeding reactions of democratic citizens and to increase the war-resisting disposition.

In such education Friends recognize for their own membership the necessity for fresh restatement and consideration of the issues. They have found that a mere tradition is incapable of giving to the next generation a stable allegiance to the negative or positive aspects of their faith. The more a small group like this shares and shares wholesomely the culture and society of its environment, the more necessary is special conditioning if it is to be nonconformist at any point, and especially when that point has the emotional and social compulsion of the military interpretation of patriotism. The continuity of Quaker witness in this area depends on recruiting from its membership and into membership stalwart believers in this particular philosophy.

While conviction on this matter follows no single procedure

of convincement or conversion, Friends have found that it comes less by argument than by personal influence and that it is more stable and more serene when it is an integral part of a fuller Christian conviction. That it can be a natural and thoroughly congenial part of a homogeneous Christian way of life is abundantly testified by experience. For many, the growth in pacifism has deepened the understanding of the Gospels. They often recall the first recorded statement of their position, the remark of George Fox when, in 1650 or 1651, he refused to secure his release from jail by accepting a captaincy in the army: "I told them," he said, "that I lived in the virtue of that life and power that takes away the occasion of wars." Effective peacemakers cannot operate in a moral vacuum. Even the negative expression is the fruit of an active and creative life and power.

The Quaker literature on the subject, whether designed for members or to influence the public, is abundant. Much of it would now be considered rather archaic, the uncritical use of isolated Bible texts, the somewhat one-sided appeal to limited considerations. Obviously, a fuller scope, a changed emphasis, is to be expected of our time, but no one can study this older literature without noting its pioneer character and the present-day relevance of many of its positions. That the use of this medium, including some of the modern extensions and applications, is one aspect of the Quaker approach to peace can be taken for granted. In the modern surfeit of the printed word it is perhaps less striking than the earlier examples.

Apart from their group and individual influence on others, what can Quakers do? Like their fellow citizens they often feel helpless in the presence of deep emotional forces tending to war. Their particular approach and their long experience should give them special responsibility, special insight, and special hope. To define and expose the forces leading to war is part of their duty. Sometimes these are economic rivalry, or the competition for markets or trade; sometimes they are racial and national feeling. Ideological factors enter in, including the older religious grouping and the new political ideologies. Militarism is a recognized breeder of war in other countries, but our own is not immune to its influence. It works through economic gain to certain industries and occupations; through the indoctrination of military service and control; through military-mindedness in government policy, in popular sentiment, in the study of history and in the fears for the future. Nationalism, sovereignty, conventional patriotism, are all breeders of war. It is the Quaker's concern to counter all these influences where he may—to help his countrymen think non-nationally on international matters, to be inventive and patient in the search for alternative procedures, and to suggest by deed and word an alternative way.

A conspicuous example has been the foreign service of Friends in recent years. Two major wars and minor ones have made the need for physical aid tragically abundant. The British Friends Service Council and the American Friends Service Committee separately and together have intervened in these situations not out of humanitarianism alone but to give expression to the positive alternative to war. Their service is not part of the war effort. In this it differs sharply from the political use of food, clothing, and technical assistance to "win friends and influence people." Its aim is to be friends rather than to win friends. It is specially concerned to cross the frontiers of hatred, suspicion, and rivalry. Its disinterestedness is to be seen when it labors on both sides of a civil war, a world war, or a cold war. Only persevering years of such experience can establish to an incredulous enemy nation, past or potential, the distinctive character of Quaker service. Here is a language other than force that can be understood by Jew and Catholic, by Arab or Hindu, by persecutor and persecuted, by fascist and communist. In such service it is particularly true that "the gift without the giver is bare."

While actions do speak louder than words, there is often more need for the freedom from fear, from hate, from despair, than for freedom from physical want. These are not instilled by wholesale, impersonal service but by a certain incarnation in individual ministrants of the "spirit of love and power and a sound mind." In proportion as Quaker service permits such contact its deeper meaning is registered. Recognition of the relevance of such service to world peace was undoubtedly the reason that the committee of the Norwegian Storting selected the service agencies of the Society of Friends for the Nobel peace prize in 1947. As was said by its chairman at the time of the award:

"Even if the statesmen succeed in constructing a better international order, it will not have a firm foundation if man has not imbibed the true spirit of fellowship. How to achieve that, is the great question.

"We know that it can be done. We have seen that a small group of people has demonstrated in a practical way the spirit which does away with the occasion of war and shown that unselfishness and goodness exist and that there are people who do not discriminate between races, between fellow countrymen and foreigners, between enemies and friends."

One way to implement the Quaker approach to peace is through the agencies of government and foreign policy. Where Friends themselves have held office they have had opportunity to exercise influence. Thus William Penn and the Quakers of Pennsylvania, so long as they controlled policies toward the Indians, avoided the kinds of war that plagued the non-Quaker colonies. In Rhode Island, their power had a similar moderating tendency. Later John Bright, the British Quaker, as a member of the Parliament and of the Cabinet, was a steadfast spokesman for peaceful policies. It is a defect in modern Quakerism that it has to so limited a degree continued the tradition of Quakers in politics loyal to the pacifism of the Society. So reasonable and abundant are the considerations of state in favor of peace that it requires no sectarian prejudice for a Friend in government to find a basis for advocating against the warlike measures of his associates those steps of policy that lead to peace. It has been said of John Bright that he "carefully and explicitly met the advocates of each war on their own ground, and showed that even on their principles it was to be condemned."

Though not in office, Friends have nevertheless a responsibility for government policy about war and peace. To implement this they work in various directions. Selecting occasions when issues that seem to them relevant are open, they attempt to elicit among their own members and persons of coinciding judgment the expression against or in favor of certain measures. For some years now continuously, as well as intermittently in the past, they have maintained an office in Washington to watch legislation on this and other matters of Quaker concern. They write or speak directly to executives and legislators in the government under which they reside, indicating the bearing as they see it of certain measures on war and peace. They testify against unlimited multiplication of armaments as creating suspicion in others; they favor limitation of armaments on a multilateral, bilateral, and even on a unilateral basis. They oppose tariff and immigration laws that seem likely to create resentment to their own country. They favor arbitration, negotiation, and peaceful settlement of international disputes. They favor world government but recognize that its success rests on general consent rather than on the threat or use of force.

Since steps like these will be effective only insofar as they reflect sincere belief in them by the government and by the people, Friends are prepared to favor such single features of this pacific policy as they can get support for from nonpacifist fellow citizens. They know that in the end the general will for peace and the willingness to pay the price for peace are essential. Without outrunning public opinion they hope to lead it as far as it will follow. They appeal for bold, patient, and untried expedients in this great cause. They know that those who support traditional military policies have reason to distrust those policies. Friends cultivate that distrust on both moral and practical grounds. But they do not expect either the nation or its rulers to adopt unconvinced the pacifist policy. Superficial allegiance is too difficult to be lasting. These difficulties Friends know full well. Yet they believe the future lies with the pacifist cause and that someone must begin. Their own vocation lies here, not as the useful challenge of a permanent minority, but as the leaven of pioneers.

This attempt to alter the official policy and the popular mind is operative, of course, at the time of crisis, but it may appropriately look backward in the chain of events attempting to deal with the remoter causes of war and not alone with the immediate *casus belli*. These are manifold. John Woolman's insight that the seeds of war are in our social order is appreciated today as never before. Friends realize the anarchy of a political alliance of sovereign states and accept in principle the ideas of William Penn's "Essay Towards the Present and Future Peace of Europe."

Suppression of free speech and free thought is recognized as only the modern successor to the religious intolerance against which Friends so effectively protested in the period of Stuart England. The connection of civil liberty with the way of peace, like that of repression with the climate of war, is obvious. Political or diplomatic policy and so military and economic policy, even if not the direct cause of war, to judge from past experience, are none the less vital in the long run. In attempting to meet the hydra-headed monster of militarism a group or even an individual naturally weighs different approaches differently. There is no reason for Friends to exclude any approach. But the method must be appropriate to the end or objective.

Besides approaching their own government officially they may intercede with foreign governments, sometimes with more welcome. This feature of individual Quaker concern has a long and interesting history and apparently some success in preventing or halting war. Whether on the mere basis of an inward sense of call, or with the additional advantage of some earlier contact and some earned right to be heard, a friendly visit to representatives of the other side should claim increasing Quaker practice. For such recent events as a mission of American Friends on behalf of German Jews to the Gestapo in 1938, or the mission of British Friends to Moscow in 1951, sufficient if inexact parallels can be found back nearly three centuries. One aim of such a mission is to mollify the war fever of one's own community as when Caleb Pusey in 1688 went right into an Indian encampment that was said to be plotting attack and found the warriors all disarmed or absent on civil pursuits, or when in 1798 George Logan went singlehanded to France and came back with terms of peace so satisfactory that the war party in the American Congress had no excuse to start a war.

The incidents of these two Pennsylvania Quakers and the recently discovered dream of John Woolman visiting unarmed the ruler of a hostile state are the precedents of more collective and more modern Quaker efforts to intervene in critical issues. Since, however, friction germinates slowly into war, many well concerned Friends try to anticipate more in advance the actual outbreak of hostilities and to bring together the rival forces in an atmosphere of understanding, or at least to acquire such friendly contact with both sides as to be able to interpret each to the other. It may not be a matter of common knowledge that at the United Nations an international group of Friends operates as a team concerned not to support any national or bloc interest but to inquire into and assist possible moves that will reduce tension and promote peace. This, and their other intimate knowledge of conditions in many countries resulting from their service there, form from time to time the basis for printed statements on the problems of cold war and of proposals toward solution.

Effective peacemaking—of the kind that Christ counted blessed—requires that one should be—to quote again His words—"Wise as serpents and harmless as doves." Were the Quakers attempting to promote "peace by pacific measures" in confidence in their own strength and sincerity alone, they would be foolhardy, naïve, and ineffective. In spite of all delay and defeat they recognize that their efforts are not solitary, irrational, or in vain. As men come more and more to recognize the irrationality, irrelevance, and immorality of war they will come to see that not any foreign nation is ever the enemy, but that war itself is the enemy and that the acquiescence of good men in it under plea of a "lesser evil" or a "necessary evil" is their own honest yet tragic alliance with the greater and unnecessary evil.

Relief and Reconstruction
BY
ROGER C. WILSON

II

Relief and Reconstruction

BY

ROGER C. WILSON

Professor of Education, University of Bristol, formerly Talks Director, BBC, and later General Secretary of British Friends Relief Service in charge of Quaker relief in England and abroad. Author of three books on Quaker relief services.

IN SPITE OF the common assumption, the Society of Friends is not essentially a relief organization or a social service agency. Its original seventeenth century title was "Friends of Truth" and it is a branch of the Christian Church, having at its heart the purpose of worshiping God and bringing men to the footstool of God and leaving them there. But because Friends have discovered and continue to discover through Christian worship that there is a steady challenge to consider and amend the social conditions in which men live, the Society has found itself taking an active part in social problems.

In the seventeenth century, Friends refused to haggle over retail prices, since they were convinced that there was a price that was fair to both parties and that it was "contrary to Truth" to exploit bargaining positions. They also pleaded for the payment of adequate living wages for day laborers. In the eighteenth century, they were well out in the forefront of the struggle against slavery, though some individual Friends were not themselves clear of slave-owning till near the century's end. In the nineteenth century, the condition of prisoners, popular education, and enlightened industrial management received Quaker attention. An organized effort for the relief of widespread suffering was begun in the Irish famine in the 1840's, continued by giving help to distressed Finns after the war with Russia in 1854–1857, and culminated with the establishment of the Friends War Victims Relief Committee to help civilian distress in the Franco-Prussian war of 1870–1871.

Down the centuries there has persisted the vital conviction that all war is contrary to the will of God, and that it is impossible for the conscientious Friend to participate in it. But that did not and does not mean that Friends have the right or the desire to stand apart from the suffering, the danger, or the boredom of wars which come from the failure of all of us, pacifists no less than participants, to work hard enough for a warless world. Faced with this gigantic failure of human relations, Friends have felt it laid upon them to try to respond by creative relief work which would call out the positive characteristics of human nature, so often smothered by the demands of war.

For a variety of reasons, the social work of Friends has tended to win the approval and support of the outside world which has come to assume that this sort of thing is the *raison d'être* for the existence of the Quakers. But to the Quakers themselves it is secondary, an outcome of the life of the worshiping church: remove the basis of worship and the sense of divine guidance, and the work would lose its mainspring. No one would deny that there is plenty of secular philanthropy in the world, much of it effective. But in Quaker experience, the philanthropy which springs from the life of a worshiping church has about it the healing touch of God himself, even though the agents be mortal and fallible men and women. Perhaps I may sum up this introduction by a quotation from a small book of mine about the experience of British Friends in relief work during and after the second world war:

> I remember talking with a member of the Service on an Aegean Island where the work was largely concerned with rather miserable refugees and the problems of settling them back, after years of purposeless demoralization in refugee camps, into the places from which they had originally come. He had been working

alongside relief workers in secular agencies, and what had impressed him was the inability of the secular workers to stand up to the sheer misery of the situation. They had come out with high ideals about the way in which society should be organized and about the part they could play. They had come out with romantic views about the way in which needy people would respond to good, sensible leading. And they had found themselves engulfed by human wreckage, by people who were wretched, dirty, quarrelsome, liars, thieves, stupid in big issues, astutely selfish in little ones, just about as unpromising a lot of citizens for the new Jerusalem as could populate the worst nightmares. In such a situation, the secular reformer and lover of his fellows found no field of service. No noticeable results could possibly follow his efforts, persistence in which led merely to failure and cynicism. Nothing, said my colleague, save Christian love, could serve in that situation to keep the relief worker sane, and to him and his fellow-workers there had come a hitherto unappreciated vitality in the Christian teaching about the way in which men are bound to one another for no other reason than their common membership in the family of God.

This attitude was not one that was met much in those who had not yet done relief work. It was an understanding that grew on the field—in evacuation hostels at home, no less than in work abroad. What weighed, perhaps, more among those contemplating service was the position of the Christian pacifist in the community. For many sensitive Christian pacifists there was no obvious clear-cut course in world war as experienced by us in this country in 1939–1945. Our conviction that all war is wrong is not based on a conviction of the absence of evil in men, though some pacifists do seem to slip into this error.

Quaker or Christian pacifism is based on an assertion that alongside man's immense capacity for sin and evil there is an eternal capacity for goodness and the things of God, and that it is only as this capacity for goodness is continually called to express itself that men, both callers and called, escape from the bonds of evil. Assertion of the supremacy of the claims of goodness over evil does not naturally make for safety or success as usually understood. The Crucifixion is a typical example of what happens when loyalty to the things of God is pursued to the end. Now, in the war, I do not think that any of us could doubt the colossal quality of the evil represented by Nazi philosophy. And

I do not think that, in political terms, it was possible to contemplate coming to any sort of political compromise with it. Political peace negotiations with Hitler were morally, no less than diplomatically, impossible. Speaking personally as a Christian pacifist, I had a far deeper sense of spritual unity with those of my friends in the fighting service, who, detesting war as deeply as I did, yet felt that there was no other way in which they could share in the agony of the world, than I had with those pacifists who talked as if the suffering of the world could be turned off like a water tap if only politicians would talk sensibly together. Where men have sinned as grievously and as long as we have done in our social and international relations with one another, there can be no easy end to the consequences. The wages of sin is death, and nothing can stop the wages being collected except the readiness shared by some pacifists and some belligerents to suffer redemptively, which is one of the paradoxically healing ways of God. In a war situation, I do not believe that we Christian pacifists have much to say on a political level, since we cannot accept the presuppositions regarding power which are so preponderant in a world at war. I believe that our obligation is:

> To love and bear: to hope till hope creates
> From its own wreck the thing it contemplates

We could not engaged in warlike activity in the hope of relieving the suffering of the Jews or of other oppressed peoples in Europe and Asia. We had, somehow, to try to participate in their suffering and to express the conviction that it is ultimately the power of suffering in love that redeems men from the power of evil. Few of us felt entirely confident that our love and imagination were of such a quality as to justify the practice of our convictions about our answer to the suffering of our oppressed fellows, especially when we remembered that many of our free fellow-countrymen were fighting and dying, amongst other reasons, for our right as pacifists to practice this conviction. And yet, for all our unclarity, we were clear that God would not have us fight. In this state of mind, many of us found ourselves drawn towards relief work with a conviction amounting to concern that this was the way God would have us respond to the failures and possibilities in which we were living.[1]

[1] Roger C. Wilson, *Authority, Leadership and Concern: A Study in Motive and Administration in Quaker Relief Work* (London: Allen and Unwin, 1949), pp. 8-10.

But while some such sense as this lay at the basis of Quaker relief work in the mid-twentieth century, the actual field-worker might express the point in rather more concrete terms:

We were to meet in the Rathaus, a red-bricked building in an undamaged suburb of the town. The warm smell of the wallflowers outside lingered as we passed through the swing doors, to be defeated by the familiar smell of municipal offices (the same in Salford or Solingen) which hung about the corridors.

We went up the stone staircase with its walls of shabby green paint to the council chamber on the first floor. On the far side of the long oval table sat nineteen German Fursorgerinnen, with the Stadtrat, an old man with white hair and whiskers, in the armchair at the head. He shook hands with our team leader and offered her a chair on his right. We followed and took the empty places opposite, eleven of us in Quaker grey.

I looked around at the leather-covered table with its heavy glass inkstands, the portraits of deceased notabilities, the Turkey carpet, the high windows, and the moulded ceiling. We might have been in Manchester, except that the Stadtrat was talking in German. We knew something of his history; he had lost his office and gone into retirement in 1933, and now, although over seventy, had returned to serve his native town. It was evidently a formal speech of welcome he was making. The Stadtrat's eloquence ended at last. It was our turn. M. spoke for us. This was not a set speech, and the atmosphere quickened. The German women leaned forward a little; all eyes were turned on her. She spoke briefly of the Quakers, of their origin and history; of the Friends Relief Service, of its work among war-victims in the occupied countries, of our own team's arrival in Germany a week ago.

"We want to help where we can, and we hope you will tell us how. That is why we want to work with you and go with you on your rounds next week. And our motive?" She paused, and in that second's pause flicked through my mind the realization that we were foreigners, British, part and yet not part of the conquering, occupying force. Would they let us help? Would they accept us? Could we do any good? "And our motive? Just the Christian one, the motive of the good Samaritan."

Three weeks later I sat in the translucent green of a late May evening, on the banks of the River Wupper, and heard from the

"Fürsorgerin" with whom I had worked something of what that Saturday morning had meant to her and her colleagues on the other side of the table. She was thirty-two and a devout Catholic. In 1933 she had been a girl at college. What the gathering darkness and horror of the Nazi regime had meant to her I was able to guess as much from her reticence as her disclosures. I could guess at the confusion of mind of one whose only source of information was the official news service, but whose principles were rooted in the gospel that there is neither bond nor free, Jew nor Greek.

Then came the collapse of Germany; and like so many others C. awoke to find that isolation was followed not by liberation but by ostracism. The world had rung with the horrors of Belsen and Buchenwald; and shame, despair, resentment and wounded pride had produced a condition of complete negativism.

Complete? Not quite. These people we had met were "Fürsorgerinnen." The name means "those who care for." They might have neither hope nor political philosophy, but they had a job to do. On each of these welfare workers depended some thousands of people, the poorest and most helpless, the old, the needy, the babies. And so, in the deepening want of postwar Germany, they took up the burden of their vocation with a courage and an integrity that commands our respect.

When their head "Fürsorgerin" summoned them to meet the English Quakers at nine o'clock that Saturday in May, they had but the vaguest idea of what they would find. Another branch of Military Government, perhaps? Some of the older ones remembered Quaker feeding after the last war; all of them recalled that school feeding introduced by Military Government had—for some reason—spontaneously been dubbed "Quakerspeisung."

What they did find was a company of amateurs with no claims to superior knowledge and no axe to grind. They resorted to metaphor in their attempt to make us realize what our coming meant to them; a breath of fresh wind; a door opened on to the world after years of imprisonment. It can all be summed up quite simply; they found that *someone* cared.

"We have been trying to help others and to give them courage out of our own bankruptcy," said C. "We have gone on in despair, feeling that our country is an outcast from civilized society, that everyone hates us, and that we have no future. It is not merely the material aid you bring, though we need it desperately. You can imagine what is is for a 'Fursorgerin' to be empty-handed when she is asked for help. But since you came I have wakened each morning without a load on my heart."

Across the river the shadows of the trees grew longer. We sat on a while in silence, willing to postpone the moment when we must pick up our bicycles and return to the half-bombed town.

"I was a hungered and ye fed me . . . naked and ye clothed me." Thus would most people epitomize the purpose of relief work. But in ruined and outcast Germany the words that came alive again, at least for me, were ". . . in prison, and ye came unto me." [2]

The relief worker who wrote this account was a schoolteacher in civilian life. She was not then, is not now herself a Quaker, but a member of another branch of the Christian Church. Her final comment sums up one central feature of the Quaker approach to relief and reconstruction. Material supplies are important, but the relief job is only half done if it has not been done in such a way as to encourage the recipient to pick up again the threads of responsible living. So often in conditions of great misery the human soul is crushed into inertia: no relief service can be more valuable than that which leads to the liberation of the human spirit.

Where large-scale material relief is essential there is no good reason why this should be done by the relief organizations of the Society of Friends. The United Nations Relief and Rehabilitation Administration—UNRRA—did a remarkable job after the second world war and showed what could be done by organized generosity on the level of government and intergovernmental administration. The Quaker contribution is best made at the level where relief workers meet, face-to-face, those in distress. Here exists that contact between persons through the experience of which both grow in understanding of what is involved in offering and receiving help. And so there has been a persistent tendency to see that Quaker relief work consists of a number of field projects with as little administrative overhead organization as possible. Only in this way can that sense of the

[2] *Social Service*, Volume XXII, No. 1. London, 1948.

supremacy of divinely ordered human relations over the claims of the administrative machine be preserved. From this it will be clear how important is the character and outlook of the individual worker in the Quaker relief service. Sheer technical or managerial ability is second to ability to get alongside other people in such a way as to encourage them to find their own solutions, even if, in the working out of them, they need material or technical help from outside. Moreover, Quaker relief work is usually done by groups and it is important that the internal relations of the group should be as free from crippling tensions as that the members of the group should be in effective relationships with those in distress. Again and again, offers of service from very able people, both within and from outside the Society of Friends, have been declined because it was believed that, for all their ability, they lacked the humility to manage human relationships sensitively. On the other hand, very ordinary people with common sense, mutual loyalty and confidence, and a deep sense of responsibility to the job can do outstandingly good work.

Here is an account of a group of seven British Friends Relief Service members (only one of whom had any professional social work qualifications) who served as the field welfare staff in the Salonika Region of the UNRRA mission to Greece in 1946. The members "did not remain as a small compact group, but worked in separate locations throughout the area, though their strong sense of responsibility to each other as well as to UNRRA gave the Regional Welfare structure of UNRRA a cohesion which it had not had before."

Each UNRRA Region compromised a number of Nomoi (i.e. Greek local government areas) and to each Nomarch there was appointed an UNRRA field advisory officer who had wide responsibility for advising the local administration on all aspects of social welfare, child feeding, the running of institutions, clothing distribution and so on. Technically, they were not executive appointments, and a good UNRRA field officer could play an important constructive part in encouraging local Greek officials to face executive responsibility with imagination and integrity—

not easy qualities to display in the uncertainties and bitter hatreds of contemporary Greek conditions.

The Salonika Region of UNRRA stretched roughly from Mount Olympus in the south to the Yugoslav frontier in the north and from the Albanian frontier in the west to the Struma River in the east, with a short common frontier with Bulgaria in the north-east. In this wild, mountainous area, with primitive communications, the Friends Relief Service team was distributed, but although widely scattered they were able because of their common tradition, training, and outlook to work together in a remarkable way. Individually, none of them would claim to have been outstandingly able—F.R.S. had few such—but as a group of hard-working, single-minded men and women, capable of trusting one another both in judgment and action in spite of isolation, and all deeply concerned to develop the confidence and competence of the Greeks without bullying or domination—as such a group the team won a remarkable reputation for first-rate work. As the Regional Welfare Director of UNRRA said, the team had three characteristics which were not universal in the UNRRA set-up: first, they worked; secondly, he did not know whether they liked the Greeks or not, but they seemed to like them; thirdly, the Greeks liked and respected them and since they took over, complaints of injustice and discourtesy from local officials and inhabitants had pretty well ceased. This was high praise indeed from a senior American officer of UNRRA in a region which had up till then been highly critical of the work of voluntary societies.

The enthusiasm of the team was impressive. Amongst other signs of this was the effort they put into learning Greek. One member was even said to talk in his sleep—in Greek.[3]

Nonetheless, while good work in the best Quaker tradition depends primarily on persons of humility, integrity, and competence, there is a need for leadership and for people with more than an average capacity for ideas. The welding of persons into effective working groups, capable of steadily pursuing complicated policies without the use of economic sanctions, is one of the most important but difficult aspects of relief work. For those who serve are volunteers, with a strong sense of vocation, paid maintenance allowances that are based on personal and family

[3] Roger C. Wilson, *Quaker Relief, 1940–48* (London: Allen and Unwin, 1952).

needs rather than on seniority, qualifications, or status. If all participating have a sense of God's leading, how should any one of them have senior administrative responsibility? The answer to this question lies in the experience of Quaker business meetings, where votes are not taken and where decisions emerge from "the sense of meeting" as it waits before God. Only against this background of Quaker method does the working of the Quaker relief group become comprehensible, with its mixture of deep democracy and firm administrative unity. Experience in the Friends Relief Service is summed up as follows:

... relief work ... involved a high measure of administrative coherence, which had to be maintained without any of the usual methods of discipline—differential rates of pay, clear grades of seniority, security or insecurity, long periods of training or, at first, a long tradition to which new-comers conformed by social pressure.

The large central core of the service had, therefore, to be people at peace with God and with themselves. These were the people with commonsense, patience, staying power, humour, and a capacity not to ask so many questions of themselves and everybody else that they could never settle down to the business of living ordinary friendly lives; they were very ordinary people so touched by the grace of God that they may be said to have been divinely ordinary, neither sentimental, nor hard, just entirely reliable and straight-forwardly intelligent, capable of spotting anything "phoney," but the sort of people whom others would instinctively trust as not being excessively clever.

The central core of ordinary people was important because wherever there were two or more members of the service working together, there was potential tension, which could easily develop to intolerable limits when there was sharp assertion of individual characteristics. In most secular situations this tension either exists and is ignored (when the job is badly done), or is avoided because the relation of the parties is purely functional, and personal factors barely enter in. But in relief work, all members were very much one of another, all shared ultimate moral responsibility equally, and very often there was virtually no possibility of physical private life. If life in the working groups was therefore to be tolerable, the majority of people had to have that natural internal peace which could treat superficial tensions at their appropriate level. The insensitive individualist, either the one who insisted on his rights, or, more frequently among us, the man who always knew what was right, could be absorbed only in very small quantities.

But while a central core of peaceful and intelligent people was essential, this alone was not enough, for the development of the Service depended very considerably on creative ideas and inspirations available to the Service through a minority. Every organization needs ideas, but no organization can stand more than a certain number at any one time, and people with ideas are often far from easy members of groups. Without our creative members the Service would have been inert, but without a large body of sensible ordinary members, the creative minds would have confused one another excessively.

The importance of a balanced environment is great, if ideas and exceptional abilities are to be used to their best advantage. For outstanding individuals are not by any means always well balanced. Imagination often resides in those with intense inner conflicts; drive in those who lack a sense of personal inner security; inspiration in those who are careless about details; capacity for understanding people in those who do not mind much about administration; administrative ability in those who think along well-set lines. Sometimes, of course, people do emerge with exceptional qualities in the desired mixture, but ability is wasted if it cannot be used when lop-sided. The more intelligently stable the group temperament, the more readily can exceptional abilities find useful and constructive scope for their expression.

Personality matters immensely in the drabness of much relief work; and the key to its preservation and growth, with a strengthening, rather than a weakening, of group solidarity, lies in the Meeting for Worship, where our individual strengths and weaknesses are caught up in the purposes of God, so that our contributions are made at a rich personal level while being rooted in a common experience which is very deep.[4]

Quaker relief work, then, is essentially service to persons, by persons, with as little obtrusion as possible of the administrative machine—which means that the administration has to be exceedingly carefully thought out and well planned in order to be unobtrusive: but that is another story. And because persons con-

[4] *Authority, Leadership and Concern*, pp. 19-21. (London : George Allen & Unwin Ltd).

tinue as children of God through all the man-made barriers of politics, race, class, and religion, Friends have always felt strongly drawn towards the assistance of those who are generally regarded as "the enemies" and who, therefore, may be neglected by secular relief agencies.

This point is not, of course, peculiar to Quakers. In 1944, when negotiations were proceeding about the conditions in which British voluntary organizations should go overseas, the Director-General of UNRRA requested that those working in UNRRA areas should wear UNRRA shoulder flashes. The British voluntary societies, secular as well as religious, unanimously rejected the request on the ground that as an agent of the Allied Governments UNRRA might lay down political conditions of relief which would oblige its staff to select this area for help and reject that, not because of need, but because of political classification. The British organizations were unanimous that, on principle, they had a universal responsibility and not one subject to Allied Government decisions, as would be implied if they wore U.N. flashes.

But British Quakers went even farther—so far, indeed, that they were prepared to leave desperate situations unmet rather than go out in what were felt to be immoral conditions. The first of these was the assumption of the British Government that relief work in liberated areas still under Allied Military Government would be done by voluntary workers wearing khaki uniforms. Since khaki was the color worn by the army, Friends believed that this would identify them with the army, a matter of grave importance to a body which was convinced that only in the spirit of Christian pacifism could the world's conflicts be rightly faced. The Friends Relief Service, therefore, felt it right to decline to participate in relief work until they were allowed to wear uniforms distinct in color from those of the army. In fact, after some delay the authorities gave permission for gray to be worn.

The second occasion was when, in the spring of 1945, General Montgomery issued a "Non-fraternization Order" forbidding informal relationships between persons of Allied nationalities and Germans in areas under his military command. The

Friends Relief Service had no desire to enter into indiscriminate, back-slapping relationships with Germans; they were well aware of the colossal problems of establishing relationships on the right basis with a country dominated by Nazis for more than a decade, and in whose name incredible horrors had been perpetrated against Jews and other Europeans, as Friends knew at first hand better than most, having worked with the consequences among refugees and in liberated countries. But Friends were not prepared to accept a situation in which their relationships with particular Germans were determined by reference to a universal military order. Even though the war was still raging, Germans continued to be persons, to be met as persons and not as an enemy class. In those circumstances, Friends again felt obliged to decline the invitation of the Military to send relief workers into Germany in spite of the desperate need, and for some weeks until the authorities accepted our reservations our workers remained waiting in Holland.

A great deal of emphasis has been placed on the method of organization and the selection of working members in Quaker relief work, because any picture of field work attempted or done would be misleading in the absence of some understanding of what lies behind it. The job itself is, in a sense, a façade; any quality or integrity it possesses comes from the corporate Christian life and experience of the Society of Friends and those who work with it.

The practical consequence of all this is that Quaker effort is usually less concerned with the preservation of physical life or the mitigation of human suffering as such—lots of other organizations find useful work in this direction—than it is with offering help in such a way that the flame of hope and constructive effort may be rekindled in human hearts. Thus, in a famine situation, the emotions are most deeply stirred by appeals to give for the children; but the policy of saving children's lives may be disastrous if the adult bread-winners are allowed to die, thus turning the children into chronic dependents until they are themselves grown up. A famine is, as a rule, a complex phenomenon and good relief work will be directed first towards steps designed for getting the area's own productive resources going again as quickly as possible and then for the development of factors which will make a recurrence less likely. This is not to say that child and other feeding programs will be ruled out. They may be essential, but only as part of a wider approach.

In Europe, after the second world war, the American Friends Service Committee devoted a great deal of effort to the establishment of neighborhood centers in badly destroyed cities so that local inhabitants might be encouraged to develop traits of neighborliness, a quality badly needed if they were to make a substantial contribution of their own toward the colossal task of reconstruction. In northern Greece, British Quakers in 1945–46 saw clearly that higher standards of living and thinking in that troubled part of the world would be much helped by the establishment of some kind of education and training for older girls from the poverty-stricken mountain villages, which for centuries had been the scene of racial, national and blood-feud massacres and arson. If the women had something to live for, maybe they would tame their men folk. And so, while UNRRA was responsible for general relief supplies, the Quaker mission developed two projects. One was a midwifery training center, where village girls would come for a three-year professional course offered free on condition that they would go back and practice in their villages for a term of years. The other was a residential domestic science school, where selected girls would be introduced in a two-year course to practical village agriculture and industry and child-care: girls usually came in small groups from the same village so that when they went back they would be able to support one another in new ways of doing things, for bad traditions die hard in the mountains of Macedonia. To this school came girls whose fathers had certainly fought one another and probably murdered one another in the terrible years of Greece's occupation and liberation.

Work camps, where young people of different nationalities or racial groups actually do a hard day's manual work together, have also loomed large in Quaker relief and rehabilitation plans. By concentrating on jobs where ideological and language difficulties are relatively unimportant, and particularly where persons of a dominant nation or race or class work on a humble equality with others, it is found that good human relationships establish a firm base from which the difficulties of ideologies, economics, and politics can be more objectively faced. These are not efforts to obscure real group conflicts, but rather to educate persons with a different experience of the same issue so that the central and intractable differences may be the more intelligently and resolutely grasped. For the same reason, relief work among students, preferably in an international setting, has been of great importance over the last thirty-five years. No political or credal tests are applied for membership in student clubs and foyers: what is hoped is that in an atmosphere of human welcome, where it is known that the organizers have no political or religious axe to grind—though they probably have strong political and religious convictions of their own—students of diverse interests will find a unity which transcends their perfectly real differences.

In overseas relief work it is essential to pay great respect to the social institutions and cultural patterns of the country in which the work is being done. In spite of increasing sociological training, foreign workers are still too prone to assume that the only method of working is that which works well at home. Highly trained social workers in particular are notoriously bad at recognizing the delicacy of the social pattern in other countries and in appreciating the need for starting on a level of unaggressive personal friendship. It is for this reason that Friends have often found that better work is done by untrained volunteers of good sense and imagination, who are prepared to learn the hard way at about the same rate as those they are supposed to be helping, than is sometimes done by highly trained people who know all the answers at home and cannot forget them abroad. This is a point that will have continually to be remembered by those who find themselves engaged in "Point Four" projects overseas. The aim is not to produce replicas of English-speaking patterns but rather to find the ways in which local initiative can work appropriately through to its own constructive patterns.

Quaker relief has come much to the fore during and in the aftermath of wars. But during the period of mass-unemployment between the wars Friends gave a good deal of thought, in France as well as in Great Britain and America, to schemes which might approach some parts of the tragedy at a human level. The major contribution of British Friends, for instance, was to establish a huge scheme for the development of "allotments" in mining areas by the provision of garden tools and supplies of good seeds. In this way many men were encouraged and enabled to do something that was useful and satisfying and so to keep their spirits alive while they grappled with major economic problems. In South Wales, it was under the leadership of Friends that a considerable number of educational settlements were started in the mining valleys, which had the effect not only of bringing good academic material to the always keen intellectual appetite of the mining population, but also of bringing outsiders into a singularly isolated and self-contained industrial area. The resulting interchange of previous experience and the sharing of contemporary South Welsh life was germinal for all parties, and personal experience gained there in the 20's and 30's has played its part in local, national, and international statesmanship, as well as at the higher levels of academic and church life.

This may all sound rather solemn and self-conscious. That is not what Quaker relief feels like to those who participate in it. There is, of course, an underlying seriousness for those who strive to devote themselves wholeheartedly to the purposes of God and have a steady purpose in life which involves disciplined living, even when, as all too often, they fall short of the vision they have been granted. But seriousness of purpose is a poor thing if it involves solemnity of manner or pomposity of expression. Work well grounded in the life of a worshiping church brings its own gaiety, even in the midst of tragedy, and to be able to laugh is as important in relief and rehabilitation as any other social skill. This comes, perhaps, especially easily in relief work staffed largely by amateurs, and without a permanent staff of veteran administrators whose self-respect is preserved partly by the inadmissibility of mistakes. For oddly enough, few experiences are more healing than a good laugh at the ridiculous consequences of well-meant miscalculations.

Economic Life
BY
KENNETH E. BOULDING

III

Economic Life

BY

KENNETH E. BOULDING

Professor of Economics, University of Michigan, author: *Economic Analysis, The Economics of Peace, A Reconstruction of Economics,* and others.

THE HISTORY OF the application of the Quaker experience in the realm of economic life presents a curious paradox. On the one hand we do not find the apparently clear-cut "testimony" which is found in the peace testimony, where a relatively simple standard of conduct has come down almost unchanged through three centuries. It is difficult to find any simple standard of economic conduct or judgment which deserves the name "Quaker." Quakers have been both capitalists and socialists, bankers and civil servants, employers and employed, masters and servants. Friends have, of course, maintained a testimony for the "minor virtues"—honesty, truthfulness, fulfillment of promises, thrift, hard work, punctuality, and so on in their economic activities as well as in other aspects of daily life. Such testimonies, important as they are, do not, however, constitute a specific attitude toward economic institutions or systems. On the great question of socialism versus capitalism, for instance, the Quaker trumpet seems to speak with an uncertain sound.

In spite of—or perhaps even because of—this apparent weakness in the clarity of the theoretical position, the practical impact of the Society of Friends on the economic life of the world has been enormous, and quite out of proportion to the small number of Friends. Indeed, it can be argued that the greatest impact of the Society of Friends on the world has been precisely in this sphere of economic life where the theoretical contribution seems to have been small. The Society of Friends has had very little influence on international relations, perhaps because of the very purity and clarity of its peace testimony. Its function in this field has been that of the prophetic voice crying in the wilderness, not that of the practical politician wrestling with the intractable problems of day-to-day conduct. This fact is not unconnected with the exclusion of Friends from positions of political responsibility (with the one notable exception of Pennsylvania) during most of their history. In economic life, on the other hand, Friends have been in the thick of things almost from the beginning, and their practical effect has been striking.

There have been two major economic revolutions in human history. The first is the development of settled agriculture and the domestication of plants and animals. This revolution may be dated about six thousand years ago and gave rise to recurrent civilizations; for once the food producer could produce more than he and his family could eat, the way was open for the development of cities and the civilizations that went with them, in both their glory and their shame. The second is the revolution in human affairs which may be dated roughly from about 1650, in the midst of which we are still living, and the final results of which no man can foresee. This is sometimes called the "technical revolution," and it involves an immense acceleration in the *rate of change* of human skills and knowledge. It is carrying man to a condition as different from his shoestring civilizations of the past as these civilizations themselves were from the condition of savagery which preceded them. Whether this new condition is one of unprecedented splendor, or whether the new revolution will carry him to extinction, nobody can say. Whatever the result, however, the old world is gone forever. And for this revolution the Society of Friends, a mere handful of people, must bear a quite disproportionate share of the praise—or blame.

ECONOMIC LIFE

The foundations of the technical revolution had already been securely laid before the Society of Friends began to make its contribution. There are two foundation stones: one is the method of scientific inquiry, the first beginnings of which go back at least to the Italian Renaissance. The other is the improvement in agricultural techniques, especially the development of root crops and artificial grasses, and the methods of "horse-hoeing husbandry." This began in the Low Countries in the latter part of the seventeenth century and was well under way in England in the first decades of the eighteenth century. It was on the foundation of the food surplus provided by this agricultural revolution that the so-called "industrial revolution" was built, and both the rise of industrial cities and the expansion of population in the western world can be attributed very largely to the improved food supplies. In this primary change Friends played little if any role, though in the later stages of the agricultural revolution the contribution of the Quaker ironmasters and especially of the agricultural implement makers such as the Ransomes of Ipswich is not to be overlooked.

The great contribution of Friends to economic improvement came in the eighteenth century in the second stage of the technical revolution, the "industrial revolution" of the textbooks. It is not the purpose of this paper to spell out the story in detail —the interested reader may be referred to Arthur Raistrick's admirable study for further details.[1] It is perhaps sufficient to mention that the basic technical changes in such industries as iron and steel, lead and zinc mining, porcelain, and even railroads were to a large extent the work of Friends. The work of the Quaker ironmasters, the Darby's and the Reynolds's, is of especial importance; indeed, the new "iron-age" would have been impossible without the discovery, by Abraham Darby of Coalbrookdale, of a practicable method of smelting iron with coal-coke, for up to this time the iron industry had been dependent on the dwindling supplies of wood charcoal.

The contribution of Friends was not confined to improvements in methods of manufacture. Friends were also active in

1. Arthur Raistrick, *Quakers in Science and Industry*. (London : Bannisdale Press, 1950).

the development of the economic institutions of the industrial age—notably in merchandising, in banking, and in insurance. The names of Barclay, Lloyd, and Gurney are sufficient evidence of the important contribution of Friends to the development of financial institutions. The abolition of "higgling" in retail trade is largely attributed to the influence of Friends. Friends also became important enough in wholesaling, especially as corn merchants, to call down upon them the wrath of that crusty old agricultural fundamentalist, William Cobbett.

It is clear that Friends have been deeply implicated in the rise of the whole set of institutional and technical changes, which go under the name of "capitalism," in two of its essential aspects—the development of a wide "market economy," and in the initiation and propagation of technical change. In these days when the institutions of capitalism are under severe challenge from the socialists and communists, and when they are also being modified almost out of recognition in response to the internal problems of a market society, as well as in response to the external challenge, it is important, though difficult, to reassess the Quaker contribution to their development. This task is of especial importance today, as the experience of the world with socialism, especially with totalitarian socialism, has thrown both the virtues and the vices of capitalism into a different relief. New insights into the nature of economic development also make a reassessment of economic history necessary, especially of the Industrial Revolution which was nothing like such a dismal affair as some historians have made out. The picture of "dark satanic mills" befouling the smiling and prosperous countryside of an idyllic past does not stand up very well in the face of what we now know about the falling death rates, the improvement in health and nutrition, and the amazing expansion in the expectation of life which follow everywhere on the heels of the technical revolution.

In assessing the Quaker contribution to economic development the question must first be asked whether this contribution is an essential and necessary consequence of the religious experience which is at the core of Quaker culture, or whether it is something extraneous, an accident of time and place not necessarily connected with the central religious experience. I shall argue that the former is the case, and that the contribution of Friends to economic life has been a very direct consequence of their religious experience, and of the organization of their religious life. The two great features of the economic life of the Society of Friends were first, the practice of the "minor virtues" or personal probity, thrift, simplicity of life, and hard work; and second, the willingness to innovate, to try out new ways of doing things, not only in manufacture and trade, but in human relations as well. The particular quality of virtue which characterized Friends, which had profound economic consequences, was a direct result of the nature of the Society of Friends as an experiment in *organized* perfectionism. It has been pointed out that the feature which distinguished early Friends from the Puritans around them—whom in so many ways they resembled —was not so much their mysticism as their perfectionism. George Fox's great objection to the Puritans was that they "pleaded for sin," and the Puritan's great objection to the Quakers was that they had the temerity to assert that a life without sin could be lived on this earth, and methodically went about organizing a society with this end in view!

The Puritans, of course, were also adept at the economic virtues, and also prospered through thrift and hard work. In this regard the Quaker testimonies and the Puritan testimonies were one. If the Quakers seem to figure in the economic history of the period quite out of proportion to their numbers, it is probably because their perfectionism offered fewer opportunities for laxity and more for experiment than the more Scripture-bound and minister-ridden life of the Puritans. The ability of Friends to survive the persecutions of the late seventeenth century, involving as they did not only imprisonment but distraint of goods and heavy fines for nonattendance at the parish church, is a remarkable testimony to the quality and the survival value of their virtues.

Even more important than perfectionism in explaining the economic contributions, however, is the doctrine and experience of the Inward Light. By resting the final authority in the Inward Light rather than in Scripture or in the church, the

Quakers provided themselves with a remarkable instrument for change. There is a world of difference between the social climate created by a traditional, sacerdotal religion in which great stress is laid on conformity to a previously given authority, and that created by a fresh, living experience of the Divine Spirit which everyone is expected to share. In the Quaker society, religion, instead of being the conservative, traditional force which it usually is, became a radical, revolutionary instrument, tearing men away from the mere acceptance of tradition to a rediscovery of the fountain of truth itself in the hearts and minds of men. "Christ said this, and the Apostles said that, but what canst *thou* say?" asked George Fox, and it is this "What canst thou say?" which haunts the whole Quaker experience. It is little wonder that such a doctrine led to remarkable innovations. In the formative years a whole new culture emerged and Friends became a "people," separated from the rest of the world by a large number of different customs not only in regard to worship, ministry, and religious organization, but in regard to marriage, lawsuits, oaths, manners (hat honor!) and many of the vital details of living. It is little wonder also that the spirit of innovation, of seeking for truth at the source, broke out also in industry and in scientific inquiry.

It is not unreasonable to conclude, therefore, that much of the impulse which led Friends to be pioneers in the technical revolution arose from within the Quaker culture itself. It must also be recognized, however, that some of the channeling of these innovating impulses came from the pressure of the world and the forces of the environment in which the little society lived. The period of the great persecutions and of the "first publishers of truth," which ended in the 1690's, was one in which the whole energies of the Society of Friends had to be devoted to mere survival. It was the energies generated in these years that produced the "flowering" of the eighteenth century. The peculiar form of the flowering, however, was determined in some degree by the disabilities which Friends still suffered even after the Toleration Act. All through the eighteenth century, and even well into the nineteenth century, British Friends were barred from the English universities by the religious tests and oaths. Consequently they were not able to follow most of the professions, medicine being about the only profession in which they engaged, thanks partly to the back door of the apothecary's trade and partly to the liberality of the University of Edinburgh. They were preserved, therefore, from a lot of the foolishness which went under the name of higher education, and were free to devote more time to the newly developing sciences and industries. The "pressure of the world," moreover, not only debarred them from certain less productive channels of activity; it forced them into a closely knit society bound together by innumerable ties of marriage and friendship, meeting together in Monthly, Quarterly and Yearly Meetings at which not only spiritual but a little worldly intercourse might take place, and new ideas, devices, and processes might be exchanged in the great family circle. The spirit of mutual help and co-operation, as well as that of innovation, contributed to the progress of techniques and of knowledge.

I have stressed the technical and scientific contributions of Friends because these are so frequently overlooked, and paradoxically enough may have exerted, and may still be exerting, a more profound influence on the course of human history than the moral and social concepts which were also a result of that probing to the source of Truth which is characteristic of the religious life. The abolition of slavery, of course, is the greatest moral and social change in which Friends pioneered. Friends were especially important in creating that initial moral sensitivity which eventually caught on among the more tough-minded evangelicals who brought the campaign in England to a successful conclusion, and inspired the even tougher-minded abolitionists of America, who fought their campaign to a somewhat Pyrrhic victory in the Civil War. The pioneering spirit of John Woolman, however, did not carry over particularly well into the nineteenth century, and once the slavery question had passed into history, it is difficult to lay one's finger on any significant moral or social change in which Friends have pioneered. Whether it was that the material success which the pioneering of the eighteenth century brought undermined the spiritual vitality of the Society, or whether the increasing formality of organization and inflexibility of tradition shut up the Society in a hard shell of its own history, the fact remains that the nineteenth century represents a low ebb in Quaker culture—so much so that in many parts of America, for instance, the Society was largely "taken over" by another kind of religious culture stemming from evangelical revivalism.

In the nineteenth century Quakerism was to a certain extent stagnant, inspiring many excellent lives in fairly traditional pattern but originating little that was new. It produced some notable individuals, like Lucretia Mott and John Greenleaf Whittier in America and John Bright in England, who made important contributions to the movements of their time, for women's rights, for the abolition of slavery or for free trade. On the whole, however, the Society of Friends contributed little towards originating or even propagating the major social movements of the day. Friends participated very little, for instance, in the struggles of the working class for a higher status in society. To this day only a small fraction of Friends has any active connection with the labor movement, whether as members or leaders. Insofar as Christianity has influenced the labor movement (and its influence has been enormous in England and America) it has done so either through the Catholic Church or through the "Methodist" type of church which apparently spoke more to the condition of working people than the more austere religion of Friends. The co-operative movement likewise, while it has attracted a few individual Friends into its orbit, does not owe very much to the Society. Politically, Friends in America are still predominantly Republican and in spite of the defection of most English Friends to the Labor Party they are mostly Liberals at heart!

The attitude of Friends toward socialism apparently reflects very diverse illuminations of the Inward Light. It is possible for ex-President Herbert Hoover, one of the staunchest defenders of capitalism, and Darlington Hoopes, 1952 Presidential candidate of the Socialist Party, both to be members in good standing of the Society of Friends. Yet looked at more closely, this dispersion is not unreasonable, but follows naturally from the nature of Quaker religion and culture. On the one hand, the urge toward brotherhood and the dominance in the Quaker ethic of the concept of universal love leads to a yearning for a familistic type of society, a reaction against the apparent impersonality and lovelessness of the market economy, and an inclination towards socialism. On the other hand, the religious individualism of the Quaker, the reaction against the collectivism of an authoritarian church, the insistence on "private enterprise" in religious experience, and the whole tenor of an "unmediated," first-hand religion leads to an uneasiness with collective action, a mistrust of the state, and a tendency to look toward individual enterprise and the market economy which fosters it as the economic counterpart of that direct approach to God which is the heart of Quaker religion. It is the tension between the Quaker ethic pulling toward collectivism and the Quaker religion pulling toward individualism which explains the wide divergence of attitude within the Society on this matter. In England the "welfare state" compromise seems to be generally satisfactory to Friends. In the United States unity on this question is much further away, and if the question is not a source of serious tension within the Society it is mainly because Friends do not extend the discipline of the group into this area of life. In politics Friends can do pretty much what they please!

What, then, of the twentieth century, and especially of its second half to which we are now looking forward? The first half of the twentieth century has seen the development of a new form of Quakerism, associated especially with the American Friends Service Committee in the United States and the Friends Service Council in Britain, and with the names of men like Rufus Jones, Carl Heath, and John Wilhelm Rowntree. It may be that the increasing external pressures brought about by the first two world wars had something to do with this revival, though clearly it began before 1914, and in many ways it seems like a true "mutation"—a rebirth of that immediate experience which is the heart of Quakerism, and its expression in the life of an organized group. It would be surprising if such a rebirth did not exert an influence in the sphere of economic life, and there are many aspects of the "New Quakerism" which reflect concern with economic problems. These impacts are not spectacular, but they may in the long run be of great significance.

The "work camp" is one of the most characteristic institutions of the New Quakerism. It is perhaps more of an educational than an economic institution, as it appeals mostly to students and young people. Nevertheless it is an experiment in creating a new pattern of work as well as a pattern of education. Though nobody at this stage is going to suggest that it is a pattern which can be extended very far, it does suggest that the nature of the group is of enormous importance in affecting individual work-motivation. In a sensé the work camp is an attempt to introduce a familylike pattern of behavior into a heterogeneous and unrelated group of people, bound together mainly by a common though temporary task. The family, of course, is the oldest and most permanent work camp! And though the family-type relationship is not applicable to large and complex organizations, experiments in social organization which involve extending the intimate and informal group relationship into the performance of economic tasks may be quite fruitful. Even more important than the development of work-camp situations may be the development of the "work-camp spirit" which derives major human satisfactions from the accomplishment of socially necessary tasks. There may be a certain danger here that young people who have found great satisfaction in the creative fellowship of the work camps may find it difficult to adjust to earning a humdrum living in a workaday world. It is important to emphasize that "service" is not something which is done only in group situations and in special and dramatic places, but that it is also the ordinary work of the world in the mine and mill and kitchen.

The interest of Friends in relief and rehabilitation has also led them into experiments in economic organization such as the allotment schemes among the Welsh coal miners, and of the Penncraft community in western Pennsylvania where miners have built their own homes and attracted new industries. A self-help housing project in Philadelphia and a farm loan scheme in Austria are included in the present economic program of the

American Friends Service Committee. If such experiments as these do not get at the heart of the economic problem, they still are a valuable expression of the Quaker genius for enterprise in the creation of more hopeful situations, especially in the area of human relations. A few Friends also have been interested in the establishment of co-operative communities, where a number of families share economic responsibilities in a more intimate way than is customary. A few others have been moved to take on themselves the burden of voluntary poverty, and to live among depressed groups such as the sharecroppers of South Carolina. On the whole, however, one must confess that the great bulk of the Society still pursues fairly conventional livelihoods—often quite successfully by the standards of the world—and has not perhaps made much distinctive contribution to the development of new economic habits, institutions, or modes of life.

It is interesting to note that with changing opportunities there has been a marked change in the type of occupation which Friends tend to select. Whereas in the eighteenth and even well up into the nineteenth century, the typical Friend might be expected to be a merchant, a small businessman, or a banker if he lived in cities, or a fairly prosperous farmer in rural areas, in the twentieth century the occupational center of gravity of the Society has been shifting into the professions—into teaching, research, medicine and out of more business-oriented or commercial pursuits. The occupational shift has been reflected also in a geographical shift: there has been a shift away from the centers of commerce and industry toward the university centers. New Friends Meetings have sprung up in university towns all over the United States, and even in England the growth of meetings at Oxford and Cambridge and the relative stagnation in some of the older industrial centers is quite noticeable. One wonders sometimes if this shift is wholly desirable—a manufacturer of agricultural machinery may do more good to the world in the long run than a producer of Ph.D.'s. Nevertheless, the shift seems to represent not only the opening up of new occupational opportunities, but also a shift in the type of enterprise which Friends favor as a life work. Also as economic life becomes more socialized in some places, we see Friends finding opportunity for their enterprise in the direction (frequently behind the scenes) of the new socialized industries. The Friend who in a previous generation would have established a business of his own may not infrequently be found as the secretary of the board of a nationalized industry!

What, then, of the future? One may doubt if the impact of Friends on economic life will ever be as great as it was in the eighteenth century. One may doubt also if Friends will produce the grandiose over-all schemes or the visible revolutions; that is not their way or their genius. It may be that one of the most important contributions will be in the field of the social sciences. The Quaker virtues are favorable to the painstaking investigation of truth. The Rowntree surveys of poverty in York were pioneering efforts in a field of social research which is growing at a phenomenal rate, and which promises to do for the social sciences what the invention of the microscope did for the natural sciences in giving them a new "eye" and an expanded view of the social universe. One hopes that the spirit of experimental living will be kept alive, and that Friends will be moved to new inventions in the whole field of human relations. It is significant, for instance, that the field of industrial relations seems to attract unusual numbers of Friends, not only as teachers and research workers but as mediators and conciliators. The recent work of the American Friends Service Committee in opening up job opportunities for Negroes, and training applicants to apply for the jobs, is a good example of a quiet but effective piece of work in a tense area in economic life.

One place where we might perhaps expect more significant developments than have in fact occurred is in the field of simplicity of life and standards of consumption. Since the almost universal abandonment of the plain dress and the degeneration of plain speech into a mark of caste, it has become increasingly difficult to distinguish Friends from the world around them, not only in their personal appearance but also in the appearance of their homes, cars, vacations, and daily lives. I write as one who has been forced to admit failure in this regard; who has found his standard of consumption creeping upwards imperceptibly with rising income until there are few, if any, outward and visible signs of whatever inward and spiritual grace he may possess. There is no sense in returning to the days when the meeting inquired carefully into the pattern of the bonnet and breadth of the hat brim, for a rigid and conservative uniformity is no answer to the problem of simplicity. Nevertheless, one cannot help feeling that conformity to the world's fashions is no better than conformity to the Meeting's fashions, and that something has been lost in the complete abandonment by the Meeting of any interest in the personal standards of consumption of their members.

In reacting against the censorious imposition of ancient and perhaps meaningless standards of consumption, we have relaxed our mutual disciplining of each other to the point where there seems to be no machinery in the usual Meeting, even for the discussion of these problems. Yet if our whole lives are indeed to be testimonies to our religious experience, it is clear that the kind of houses we live in, the kind of clothes that we wear, the kind of vehicles that we use, the kind of hospitality we indulge in, and the kind of property that we own often speak in louder, clearer tones than the words we say. If there are areas of life into which we do not admit the light of the Spirit, that light itself will dim upon us. It is for no man, of course, to prescribe for another what he should do, or how the leaven of the spirit should operate in his life. If one feels called to earn a fairly comfortable, conventional income and to live in a house that permits the exercise of hospitality, it is not for another to criticize him. One would also like to see, however, the growth of more spartan and spiritually athletic groups, living a life stripped of all nonessentials, a little more aloof from the "world" than the rest of us, experimenting in many kinds of new modes of living and standards of consumption. This is of particular importance to American Friends, who so often slip into a dependence on high standards of consumption which unconsciously alienates them from people in less fortunate parts of the world.

An area of economic life which particularly touches the conscience of Friends is that of involvement in war and warmaking activities. This problem has been becoming increasingly acute as war and the war economy penetrate deeper and deeper into the lives of the people. Curiously enough it is the technical revolution itself which is mainly responsible for this constant encroachment of the military on the civilian economy. A poor society cannot afford to devote more than a fraction of its resources to war. By far the major part of its economic effort must be devoted simply to keeping itself alive, to raising the basic necessities of food and clothing. As a society improves in its productive powers, however, it becomes able to produce its basic necessities with a smaller proportion of its total population, and hence more of its people are liberated for other tasks, whether for building pyramids, fighting wars, or raising the general standard of life. If the political structure implies competition in armaments, the inherently insatiable demands of national defense under these conditions produce a drive toward absorbing resources in defense up to the maximum which the society can afford. In a poor society this will be only a small proportion of its resources. (Thus Adam Smith in the late eighteenth century believed that no modern nation could have more than one per cent of its men under arms without bankrupting itself.)

In a society like the United States, however, it is perfectly possible to devote one-half, or perhaps even three-quarters of the national income to war and armaments, and if the competitive defense situation demands it, such as a struggle between two approximately equal powers, the possibility may become actual. Consequently it is much more difficult for a person to achieve noninvolvement in war in a rich than in a poor society. Conscription is one sign of this increasing proportion of resources devoted to war. A poor society could not afford the large armies raised by conscription, and can easily raise by voluntary enlistment the small armies which it can afford. Even more difficult to avoid than conscription, however, is involvement in war industry, where such a large part of the industrial machine is in fact war potential.

An economic issue which has concerned some Friends in this connection is tax refusal—the attempt to withhold from payment that part of taxes which it is estimated is spent for war purposes. It may be doubted whether tax refusal makes such sense as an economic strategy since it does not particularly affect the proportion of resources which goes into the war industry. Government generally has powers to distrain property for taxes, so that the tax refuser frequently pays more in the end, and it also has the ability to create money which gives it the power to attract resources to itself even if no taxes were paid at all. The result of such procedures would, of course, be inflation, which in itself is a form of taxation, and an unfair and unjust one. Indeed, the main purpose of taxation is to prevent inflation, rather than to "pay for" government expenditure in the conventional sense. This does not mean that tax refusal as a symbolic act of protest under Divine Guidance does not have a place in the scheme of things; it must be judged, however, in its aspect as symbolic act, and not as a means of influencing the economy.

Any attempt to summarize the Quaker contribution of economic life must appear rather disjointed and fragmentary. There is no single clear principle by which the contribution may be characterized. Nevertheless, if the religious life of the Society continues to flow strongly, Friends will continue to play a part, even if a modest one, in the development of economic ideas and institutions. There are two great concepts around which the life of Quakerism revolves: enterprise and brotherhood. The spirit of enterprise is that which leads into more knowledge and power, and into better ways of doing things, whether producing an article or producing fellowship and community spirit. It leads into social experiments of all kinds by seeking out better ways not only of making things but of living together. The spirit of brotherhood leads into peaceableness, into the search for ways of reducing tensions, and of eliminating oppression in all its forms. It sees economic and social life as an essentially co-operative structure, an arrangement for mutual aid. It goes beyond this and sees society as an expression of love and concern of all for all, in which the needs of those who cannot contribute are met as well as the needs of the contributors.

Between enterprise and brotherhood there should always exist a creative tension. It is enterprise which leads to wealth and power, not only for the individual but for the society as a whole. Without enterprise, brotherhood is an impotent sentiment. Without brotherhood, however, enterprise leads to oppression and wealth leads to damnation in the satisfaction of inferior desires. This is true under any kind of economic or social system. And separated from God, separated from the sensitizing of the spirit in worship and communion with the source of all love and truth, enterprise leads to damnation in pride, brotherhood leads to damnation in sentimentality. This remains the most important thing which the Society of Friends has to say, even in the field of economics.

Business and Industry
BY
D. ROBERT YARNALL

IV

Business and Industry

BY

D. ROBERT YARNALL

President, Yarnall-Waring Company, manufacturers of power plant specialties, Philadelphia; Mechanical Engineer.

WHEN THE QUAKER colonists started from England on their journeys to Pennsylvania, about 1683, George Fox told them to "keep your own plantations in your hearts with the spirit and power of God that your own vines and lilies be not hurt." Many of these Quaker businessmen were successful over the next three-quarters of a century in "making outward plantations."

Their religion, which was part of their daily life, made for success. "Their yea was yea and their nay was nay." They would not "cozen or cheat." They established a one-price policy in merchandising and stuck to it through thick and thin. And behold, their businesses prospered. But with outward success, many Friends became entangled in outward responsibilities which almost inevitably led to compromises and which in turn ultimately affected the spiritual integrity of the Society of Friends.

In this colonial period of successful and influential Philadelphia Quaker businessmen there was a growing uneasiness in the Society which was perhaps most vocal through the preaching and visiting among Friends of John Woolman of Mount

Holly, New Jersey. He was a successful businessman himself—a tailor by trade, a merchant, a conveyancer, and a skilled grafter of fruit trees. He had a very sensitive conscience and was troubled by his growing outward success. He records this struggle of mind in his *Journal:*

The increase of business became my burden, for though my natural inclination was towards merchandise, yet I believed Truth required me to live more free from outward cumbers. There was now a strife in my mind betwixt the two, and in this exercise my prayers were put to the Lord, who Graciously heard me, and gave me a heart resigned to His Holy will; I then lessened my outward business.

John Woolman also expressed concern and sympathy for those other Quaker rich men "who have at times been affected with a sense of their difficulties, and appeared desirous . . . to be helped out of them," yet for want of abiding under the humbling power of Truth, continue to be entangled in outward cumber.

One wonders what William Penn, who died in 1718, would have counseled. We may remember what he said about "True godliness" in his book *No Cross, No Crown,* printed in 1682:

True godliness does not turn men out of the world, but enables them to live better in it, and excites their endeavors to mend it. Christians should keep the helm and guide the vessel to its port, not meanly steal out at the stern of the world, and leave those that are in it without a pilot, to be driven by the fury of evil times upon the rock or sand of ruin.

To move quickly from the past and the philosophies of George Fox, and John Woolman, and William Penn, what of the current situation in which Quaker businessmen find themselves in 1952? The Society of Friends has grown in numbers, but much less rapidly than the rate of growth of the national population.

In times past, Friends were largely engaged in farming and enjoyed a good degree of economic independence and the other fruits of rugged individualism. In the past half century, however, business pursuits have claimed a growing majority as more and more families have moved to the city. Quaker members in the main seem to be successful in their enterprises—whether as farmers or as businessmen or as professional people.

The Society—due to the faithfulness of Friends of the past as well as of the present—seems still to have spiritual vitality in our day, but also enjoys a degree of acceptance by non-Friends which embarrasses many concerned members. Each year the Society formally asks Meetings to consider certain Queries which keep before members recurrently its deeper concerns and aspirations. Here are four from the Philadelphia Yearly Meetings which bear particularly upon the lives of members engaged in business:

(a) What are you doing to create a social economic system which will so function as to sustain and enrich life for all?
(b) What are you doing to carry your share of responsibilities in the government of your community, state, and nation, and to assure freedom of speech and of religion and equal educational opportunities for all?
(c) Are you careful to keep your business and your outward activities from absorbing time and energy that should be given to spiritual growth and the service of your religious society?
(d) In all your relations with others do you treat them as brothers and equals?

Although in these Queries one recognizes some of the deep concerns of George Fox, William Penn, and John Woolman, there is also a new emphasis. Here we recognize the persistent and living concern of the Social Order Committee of the Philadelphia Yearly Meetings, which for forty years under the leadership of Bernard G. Waring and a host of other devoted witnesses has focused attention upon old and new social concerns.

All these are impelling reminders which help to keep before Quaker businessmen in this generation those spiritual values which are beyond the profit motive—values which would help control the acquisitive instinct.

What kind of Quaker businesses do we find today? In England three prominent chocolate manufacturing firms come first to mind—Cadbury, Fry, Roundtree—as well as heavy industries and various kinds of manufacturing.

In the general Philadelphia neighborhood there are many successful businesses founded by Quakers and in most of them today we find concerned Quaker management. They include:

Department stores	Engineering and architect firms
Iron and steel foundries	
Instrument manufacturing	Accounting and auditing firms
Glass works	Leather goods
Power plant equipment manufacturing	Printing
	Chemical manufacturing
Automatic machine manufacturing	Insurance companies
Dairies	Banks and trust companies
Hotels	Hospitals

These are examples of successful enterprises, but also examples of good and concerned industrial relations. Seebohm Rowntree (now in his eighty-third year), a distinguished British Quaker industrialist, when visiting this country in the autumn of 1951 said to a group of Quaker businessmen, in part:

Industry should create goods, or provide service of such kinds, and in such measure as may be beneficial to the community. In the process of wealth production, industry should pay the greatest possible regard to the general welfare of the community, and pursue no policy detrimental to it.

The life of the community depends on industry; therefore it is important that industry should be efficient and waste should be reduced to a minimum. Greatest source of waste arises through lack of cordial cooperation between employers and employed. Our aim should be to induce all to work as hard and as intelligently as if they were working for themselves.

Both in the United States and in England, we take pride in the fact that ours is a democratic nation. Our political system is democratic, but it is largely true that democracy stops at the factory gate. It is necessary to establish basic conditions in industry which are just and which take full account of the changed outlook of the workers, and secondarily to see that all administrative acts are carried out in the right spirit. An overbearing foreman or manager, while conforming to the letter of admirable regulations, may fail to get the desired cooperation.

Remember there is no such thing as "Labor." The working force is made up of a number of individuals each having a personality different from the rest. They are sensitive as we are to encouragement and discouragement, as easily aroused to anger and suspicion, to loyalty and to effort. Put the *best man* in the works in charge of labor, the man with the biggest heart and the wisest head. Don't minimize the labor side of the business.

And lastly let us not forget a warning uttered by Tolstoy: It all lies in the fact that men think there are circumstances in which one may deal with human beings without love; and there are no such circumstances. One may deal with things without love; but you cannot deal with men without it, just as one cannot deal with bees without being careful. If you deal carelessly with bees, you will injure them, and will yourself be injured. And so with men.

Concerned Quaker businessmen, feeling that labor and management should better understand each other's point of view, arranged two conferences, one in 1950 and the other in 1951. The particular subject for the first one was a report of Quaker economists which was distributed in advance to about twenty businessmen. Perhaps the underlying question of the conference might be stated thus: Where does our religious responsibility lie in the conflict between "take home pay" and the margin of profit needed in industry?

Agreement was expressed with the statement of the economists that labor unions are essential, particularly in large industries. They were felt to be essential as a means of communication between management and workers. We were reminded that communications are often as poor in a small firm as in a large one. Viewpoints are bound to differ, irrespective of the size of a company. Both sides must get together and place facts on the table honestly, and more important than mechanical arrangements is the spirit in which negotiations take place.

In considering what the distinctive Quaker contributions could be, there was suggested a similarity between the Quaker business meeting and collective bargaining at its best. Negotiations on this basis can result in a higher synthesis of the different points of view, rather than the lowest common denominator. It was pointed out that the Quaker Meeting presupposes a certain equality and simplicity which would have to be brought into industrial relations.

The second conference, in 1951, was composed of 44 representatives: 17 union leaders and workers, 19 from management, 6 from education, 2 miscellaneous. Shortcomings of management and the labor unions were freely and helpfully discussed by experienced leaders in both groups. The conference also emphasized that top management must take responsibility to see that lower management is properly selected and trained; and union leaders must see that the workers and stewards understand and follow the agreements.

In response to questions from the businessmen present, the labor representatives stated that the objectives of the union are to protect the dignity and the standard of living of the worker, to secure for him a fair share in the product of industry and a voice in the business in which he works. Insofar as the union has a general philosophy, it aims to develop industrial democracy. "A fair share" was described as the most that management can pay and carry on the business.

After the second conference, some of those present mentioned that they were aware for the first time of the possibilities inherent in the increasing participation of labor unions in matters formerly thought to be the sole prerogative of management.

As a result of the two conferences, one has the impression that much good may come from friendly discussion of common labor-management problems at a time and place removed from the often hectic atmosphere of the collective bargaining table.

It was apparent from the conferences that some Quaker businessmen have come to realize that the "union" is not a thing of evil as it used to be considered, but rather is now a door of opportunity for concerned and honest workers and management to work out co-operatively rules of procedure upon which the industry may produce goods acceptable to the consumer at a fair price as far as labor costs are concerned which will adequately take care of all of the factors involved.

One of the Quaker companies with an over-all working force of about three hundred had just completed a labor-management agreement which when reviewed gave quite a characteristic picture and understanding of the scope of hundreds of such contracts which are quietly negotiated each month throughout the year in every industrial community in the United States.

Management has many financial responsibilities other than that of meeting the payroll each week: sales expenses related to order-getting, advertising, research and development expenses, bonus incentives, pensions, dividends to stockholders, inventory, financing, taxes, and reserve for future security of the business. It is most important to bring these hard facts to the fore, in order to develop and keep alive a "sense of community" —what is good for one is good for all.

During the last thirty years, great changes have been developing in the business world, and of late it would seem they are coming at an accelerated pace . . . and the end is not yet.

1. The separation of ownership and control in businesses in our day involves a change in the organization of enterprises almost as revolutionary as that which occurred in the industrial revolution in the early eighteen hundreds.

2. The corporate system is now bringing a change in the position of capital much as the factory system changed that of labor. A typical case in point is the General Electric Company with 250,000 stockholders and 190,000 employees.

Who are the owners of the company? Who controls the management?

3. Another change that is taking place—and one having serious implications—is that smaller successful businesses are being sold to larger businesses because very heavy inheritance taxes must be paid by survivors.

4. Increasingly heavy taxation by federal, state, and municipal governments is making it more and more difficult for key employees to acquire and hold on to participating shares in their company, because a high percentage of their year-end

bonuses must be paid in taxes. However, it may be that this will result in their investing in more conservative investment shares of their companies and in the end they may be better off.

This brief description of some of the parts and problems which make up successful enterprises in our generation may seem to some complicated and forbidding. To one looking at the picture from the inside, however, it presents a door of opportunity to young men which is not related to "the leadings" which our fathers and great-grandfathers and great-great-grandfathers had presented to them.

Each year a few young Quaker businessmen start their own businesses. Some have rough sledding and do not come through, while others are able to meet their competition and forge ahead into a position of satisfying stability.

Other Quaker young men—the great majority—elect to cast their lot with established businesses and make their contributions through the innumerable jobs available. Many are attracted by the challenge in industrial relations and personnel departments, believing that only here can they find the channels through which to express their social concerns. This is a worthy ambition, but it is well to remember that economic justice and harmonious human relations cannot be synthesized in any enterprise by a special department set up for the purpose; instead, these principles must be rooted in every corner of the organization. Hence, any concerned person, no matter what his position, can find important opportunities to apply his social and economic concerns to his day-to-day job.

Right here it might not be amiss to remember the experience of Brother Lawrence, who, resolving to devote himself to the service of God, entered a monastery; but instead of spending his time in meditation and psalm-singing, he was sent to the kitchen—"being a dull and stupid fellow"—to cook for the rest of the community. He was greatly cast down; how could he practice the presence of God in a noisy room with people rushing about all shouting for different things?

Then came the answer—"Nothing is easier. I have but to turn the cake in the pan for the love of God."

He learned to offer up every humdrum duty as an act of worship, and thus the kitchen, not the cathedral, produced one of our finest Christian classics.

How far can we go in building "outward plantations" and remain within the bounds of Quaker procedures?

Some businessmen will follow George Fox and reduce their efforts in building "outward plantations" and turn within. A few, perhaps only a small percentage, will spurn "the accumulation of cumber," as did John Woolman. They will sell their businesses and devote their lives to spiritual pursuits. The larger number of men in business, members of the Society of Friends, mindful of the Advices and the Queries and the social responsibilities which are laid upon them recurrently, will most likely move in the direction of William Penn's advice in *No Cross, No Crown:*

True godliness does not turn men out of the world, but enables them to live better in it, and excite their endeavors to mend it. . . .

The more spiritually sensitive taking this course will say to themselves: "The acid test of the rightness of my course will be found in the answer I am able to make to that Query which is the summation of all Queries—'Are Friends responsive to Divine promptings?'"

May we remind ourselves that we will only lift the climate of American business life in our generation if our own lives are deepened and lifted up.

Education
BY
HOWARD H. BRINTON

V

Education

BY

HOWARD H. BRINTON

Director of Pendle Hill, graduate Quaker school, Wallingford, Pa., from 1936 to 1952. Author of more than a dozen books in the fields of Religion and Education, most recent, *Friends for Three Hundred Years.*

By education we ought to understand whatever has a tendency to invigorate the intellect, to train the mind to thought and reflection, to mould aright the affections of the heart and to confirm us in the practice of virtue.[1]

THIS DEFINITION expresses the ideal of Quaker education as it was envisaged a hundred years ago and it continues to serve as the ideal in Quaker schools and colleges today. The four objectives are really two, each being mentioned twice. According to this statement, education must include the development of both mind and heart, training in the use of the intellect and practice in the ways of virtue. In other words, education is concerned with both thought and feeling.

Much of education today is focused more upon the first; that is, on thought, intellect or reason. There is too little conscious cultivation of the kind of wisdom which comes through feeling. By feeling I do not mean emotion which may accompany any kind of activity, but rather that capacity by which we discover

[1] Dorothy L. Gilbert, *Guilford, A Quaker College* (North Carolina: Guilford College, 1937), p. 77.

what is valuable in itself. That which is valuable as a means toward some particular end is ascertained by reason, but the value of the end itself is made known by feeling. A good life is worth living for what it is in itself, not for what can be done with it, and the character of a good life is realized not through any process of reasoning, but by our deepest feelings.

The worship of God, if genuine, is valuable for what it is in itself. If I worship God or live a good life because of some benefit which I may receive from doing so, I am neither sincere nor genuine. If I write a poem or paint a picture, I would like you to enjoy or value it for what it is in itself, not for what you can do with it; in other words, I would hope that it might inspire you with the same feeling that I enjoyed in creating it. If you commend my creation because it possesses admirable qualities, and yet you do not have the right experience on being exposed to it, very likely I have failed. I appeal to your critical judgment, but the criterion of taste is not made by reason. It is an act of appreciation made by the feelings. We spend much time, and rightly, on educating powers of thought by which we judge what is true or false, but how can we educate the feelings which tell us what is good or evil, agreeable or disagreeable, religious or irreligious, beautiful or ugly; in other words, how can we educate the sense of value?

We provide in our colleges courses in philosophy, literature, ethics, aesthetics, and religion. These subjects involve taste and judgment of value by means of feeling. But our college courses in these subjects are often as intellectual in content as are courses in mathematics. Even in theological schools this condition prevails. Students are provided with theories which various authorities have advanced regarding the nature of, shall we say, religion. They give a knowledge about the subject, not the knowledge of acquaintance.

In a course in science the teacher undertakes to help his students to become scientifically minded, but in a course in religion the teacher does not necessarily undertake to help his students to become religiously minded. There are no laboratories in religion where the students seek to attain to religious experience. In ethics the student may learn what various thinkers have thought about the nature of good and evil, but is he thereby inspired to be good? He may even feel, since the great authorities disagree regarding the nature of what is excellent, that goodness is purely relative to one's interest and point of view. A student who is morally bad might receive the highest grade in ethics, and a student might be given a grade of A in aesthetics who had never experienced a genuine feeling for the beautiful. Without a true feeling for the good, the beautiful, the religious, knowledge in these fields is intellectual.

I do not wish to be misunderstood as identifying the good, the beautiful, and the religious. Feeling gives us wisdom in many different fields, including humor. It would be possible for a man without any sense of humor to write a book on the subject simply by observing what kinds of things people laugh at. He would have an intellectual or scientific knowledge of humor, but not a basic feeling for it. In the same way it would be possible for a deaf man who had never heard a sound to write a book on sound. Most laboratory experiments on sound involve principally the use of the eyes in reading chart recordings.

In scientific studies we learn of facts and theories regarding the world revealed to us by our senses. These facts may be used for a good or an evil purpose; education in facts alone is an incomplete training. We are now beginning to realize that the belief in progress through scientific knowledge, so characteristic of the nineteenth century and the early decades of the twentieth, is an insufficient, if not a false belief. It used to be taken for granted that humanity was getting better and better because we knew more and more. Every new discovery in science increased the sum total of human knowledge. The age of optimism was ended by the two world wars and the rise of totalitarian states in which scientific knowledge was used for the opposite of good purposes. It is clear now that increase in scientific knowledge may increase man's power to do evil as it may increase his power to do good.

Some persons, who realize that recent and still continuing tragic events demonstrate how science destroys as well as builds and heals, tell us that our trouble is due to the fact that the physical sciences are overdeveloped in comparison with social sciences. We know too much about nature and not enough about man. The balance will be restored if we develop biology, economics, sociology, and psychology as elaborately as we have developed physics and chemistry. These critics do not realize that the social sciences are often pursued in a way that is just as intellectual and as little concerned with value as are the physical sciences.

A dictator who wishes to exercise absolute control over his people needs a keen knowledge of social psychology in order to make his propaganda succeed, of sociology in order properly to organize his supporters, of economics in order to make prosperity appear entirely dependent on himself, and of biology in order to breed a race with a slave mentality. The laws of heredity enable a breeder to breed pigs so fat that they are unable to walk. This may be a satisfactory result from the farmer's point of view, but an unsatisfactory result from the point of view of the pig. Expertness in social sciences might be useful to those in control, but its misuse might prove the opposite to those who are controlled. Does this mean that we should give up education as a means of improving mankind? The answer I wish to emphasize is this: Education should be more ardently pursued than ever before, but it must be an education of feeling as well as an education in thought.

Does goodness come through knowledge? Can virtue be taught? These are very old problems. They were discussed at length by Plato in *The Republic* and have often since been subjects of debate. I believe that virtue does come through knowledge and can be taught, but not through an intellectual knowledge of facts so much as by a knowledge of values obtained through sensitizing our feelings, particularly our consciences. Thinking may tell us what is true or false, but only feeling—in this case we call it conscience—can tell us what is right or wrong. No one was ever argued into being good. A person becomes good by apprehending goodness in the depth of his soul at the spring of his will. Thoughts are on the mind's surface. Feelings arise out of what may be called the depths. It is not easy to reach those depths by any conventional method of teaching. Von Hugel writes, "It is by the apparently slight, apparently faraway accompaniment of a perfectly individual music to the spoken or sung text of the common speech of man, that I am, it would seem, really moved and won."

Psychologists tell us that we seldom do things because of reasons for doing them. More often we find reasons for doing what we want to do. Feelings influence thought in a way we do not usually realize. We all experience fears, dislikes, and prejudices which run counter to our reason. It is quite possible for thought and feeling to be on opposite sides of a question. Some persons, for example, who are pacifists in their thoughts, act in a way which indicates that they are warlike in their feelings. Some who are militarists intellectually may be pacifist in their feelings and quite incapable of becoming effective soldiers. Some, by a process of logical reasoning, become opposed to all racial discrimination, but they are obviously possessed by feelings which are discriminatory. This is shown when they go so far as to overemphasize their good relations with minorities.

A certain group of communists in England a few years ago agreed to practice their theories and live together communally. When they got together they quarreled over each person's share of work and goods. It was soon found better to separate. These people were communist in thought but individualist in feeling. I remember that in my college days our professor of economics, like other professors of economics, was a free-trader and convinced us of the soundness of his position, but all his students who went into business immediately became advocates of a high tariff.

Is there then any method of education which will educate feeling as well as thought so that the two will be in harmony? If thought and feeling are not in harmony, man is at war with himself; and if he is at war with himself, he will soon be at war with others.

At a musical concert Sir William Crookes, the famous physicist, was once asked, "Why are you so interested in that man's playing?" He answered, "I was merely seeking to calculate the energy in foot-pounds being expended per minute." This answer indicates the nature of a problem which faces us today in many forms, a problem arising out of the fact that we are all specialists. We are apt to specialize either in thought or in feeling, seldom in both. Hence, we are out of balance. It is not considered correct for a professor of one subject to take more than an amateur's interest in other subjects.

When Sir Arthur Eddington, the famous Quaker mathematical physicist, wrote about mysticism, he forfeited the confidence of some of his fellow physicists. Since the sixteenth century, human knowlege has become so vast that no one can claim to compass more than a very small part of it. As a result, learned men tend to be one-sided. A specialist in a subject involving thought would hesitate to specialize also in a subject involving feeling; he would probably figure that he had not the capacity to do both. If he specializes in thought, his feelings remain undeveloped, and immature. A businessman who has spent his whole life in making money may realize, when he is about to retire, that he has no religion and that he needs what religion alone can give if his life is to have a satisfactory goal and meaning. He goes in for religion and not infrequently adopts fantastic, even infantile, religious ideas because up to now his religious feelings have remained undeveloped.

Our whole culture is out of balance because its attention has become concentrated on tools and machines, products of intellect, rather than on the goals and meanings which can be ascertained only by feeling. We make extremely efficient automobiles in order to go nowhere in particular. We are concerned with means rather than with meaning, with tools rather than goals. Our civilization is a tool civilization.

It may be that human beings first began to have self-conscious, logical thought processes only when they began to create tools. The animal whose tools grow on his body does not, because of them, develop self-conscious thought. His tool-using arises out of his subconscious feelings. We are grateful for the development of reason by which the human race has reached pre-eminence in the animal kingdom, but the penalty often paid for this advance is the underdevelopment of feeling and the inability to realize value.

In certain respects human beings have reached the prominent place they hold for the very reason that men are in many ways less highly specialized than animals. It has been remarked that a human hand is not as useful as a wing for flying, a fin for swimming, or a claw for fighting. But the hand is more useful than any of these because it is so generalized and so sensitive to a variety of situations. Though it cannot be used for flying or long-range navigation, it can produce airplanes and ships. Perhaps we can learn from our own history as human beings that, while specialization is one of our greatest advantages, we misuse it at our peril. All sides of our being must be both efficient and responsible.

So far we have only diagnosed our difficulty, and diagnosis is easier than cure. How can we educate feeling? How, for example, can we teach religion, a question which Sunday school teachers ask in despair? It is not difficult to teach facts about religion, its history, its doctrines, its practices, but that is very different from making even the earnest student religious. The Quakers have been clearly aware of this problem and of the nature of its solution.

The founders of the Society of Friends discovered the Inward Light which came from God and shone into their souls. Their discovery was not new. Christians had previously been aware of the Divine Spirit giving strength and guidance from within; especially were the early Christians aware of it, first at Pentecost and many times later when the Spirit was poured out upon congregations. But in the seventeenth century it was not generally realized, and the Quakers' emphasis on it was considered to be a revolutionary doctrine. At that time the Protestants held that moral and religious truth could be found only in the Bible; the Catholics held that the Church was the sole repository of such truth; while, then as always, there were many who thought that morality and religion could be deduced by a process of reasoning.

The Quakers denied the primacy of all three of these sources of religious and moral truth, though they acknowledged the value of each as an important secondary source. They held that the fountain of truth was man's deepest feelings resulting from the permeation of his soul by the Divine Spirit, which they called the Inward Light. This Light is not primarily revealed on the surface of the mind, where are the ideas which we use in dealing with our outward environment. It shines into the depths of the soul and it can be reached only by "centering down," to use an old Quaker phrase: that is, by concentrating our attention on the inward side of life where the soul's windows open toward the Divine, rather than on the outward side where the windows open toward the world revealed by our senses. This Light Within coming direct from God can tell us what is ultimately valuable. Reason, church tradition, and the sacred book, all of them derived from the Light, provide indispensable checks on the character of our guidance.

To the Light the Quakers ascribed other functions besides that of revealing moral and religious truth. It was the Light which gave man power to act on his religious and moral insights and brought him into unity with God and his fellow men. The Light could move the will in a way which reason could not. This is another way of saying that the Light is apprehended by feeling rather than by thinking. The highest religious activity is simply opening the soul to the Light in the silent, waiting expectancy of worship.

For this reason the early Friends hesitated in regard to higher education, lest so much study result in a religion of ideas rather than in a religion of feeling. They were opposed to what they called "airy notions" or a religion "afloat on the surface."

William Dewsbury, one of the most saintly of the early Friends, wrote in a letter:

> I have a concern upon my spirit to write to you that you do not rest in an outward profession of truth received by education, but watch into the heart-searching Light of Christ in you which will let you see that you must be regenerated and born again and so be made real and faithful Friends by the heavenly inspiration of the Spirit of God in you.

And in a similar vein William Penn wrote that for

> most men . . . that which is the religion of their education and not of their judgment is the religion of another and not theirs.
> (*Fruits of Solitude,* Works, p. 742)

Friends knew, however, that Quaker children, if they were to be useful citizens and succeed in life, must know how to read, write, keep accounts, and speak grammatically. They even needed to learn foreign tongues in order to be able to spread the Truth. So, where a meeting house was built, an elementary school was also established. But Friends soon found that it was not easy to get teachers of high character, qualified to exert the acceptable kind of religious and moral influence on their students. The boarding schools, set up by several Yearly Meetings, resulted, partly at least, from an effort to prepare teachers for the elementary schools. Particular efforts were made to secure the right kind of environment to educate students religiously and morally. Of the first 400 students at New Garden Boarding School, 100 became teachers.

But Friends were then faced with the problem of securing the right teachers for the boarding schools and also for the Quaker academies, many of which were founded in the first half of the nineteenth century. As a result of this demand (though there were other reasons as well), the Quaker colleges evolved, having, in a sense, the same objectives as the boarding schools. In the initial stage the colleges resembled the boarding schools and academies in many ways. This was natural and inevitable in the case of Guilford, Haverford, and Earlham which developed directly out of the boarding school. Swarthmore College was founded because of the concern of Benjamin Hallowell that better teachers be prepared for Quaker schools.

By the nature of their need of teachers, Friends were induced to undertake higher education though they continued to have reservations about it. In the course of time it became clear that their hesitation was not in regard to higher education as such, but toward the particular kind of higher education that was concerned with words and ideas to the exclusion of training and experience having to do with acts and feelings. As the Guilford College Trustees expressed it, there must be an education of the heart as well as the mind, a training in virtue as well as intellect. Allen Jay, who once raised money for Friends' colleges, quotes in his *Journal* a speaker who said:

The Quakers have the true idea of education. They educate the body, intellect and heart together, which is the true system of education, for if you educate the intellect alone, you have a cold and formal Christian, or if you educate the heart and emotions alone, you have a fanatic with his hobbies.

Job Scott, a Quaker schoolteacher, writes:

I fear a great part of the tuition which too many children receive under the name of Christian instruction tends rather to blunt the true sense and evidence of divine truths upon the mind and to substitute notions and systems instead.

The Quaker emphasis on feeling rather than doctrines, creeds, or arguments as a source of moral and religious truth is well illustrated by typical expressions used in Quaker meetings for the transaction of the business of the church. A conservative Quaker who is still under the influence of the older customs will not say, "I believe this to be right"; he will say, "I feel this to be right," "I feel that I must go on this journey," "That course is in accord with my feelings." An examination of the Quaker journals or autobiographies shows the wide use of the word "feel" in reference to any concern that the writer apprehends has been laid upon him.

How then did the Quakers undertake to teach religion and morality?

The boarding schools were in their early days almost all of junior college rank. Many subjects were taught, such as Christian Evidences, the Principles of Morality, Philosophy, Logic, Analytic Geometry, Trigonometry, Astronomy, Navigation, Surveying, which today might be studied in the first or second year of college. In North Carolina, for example, there was New Garden Boarding School under the Yearly Meeting and about ten academies under Quarterly Meetings, the latest survivors being Belvedere (1834–1914), Woodland (1876–1916), and, near by in Virginia, Corinth (1888–1908).

These educational institutions were organized on the family plan. They were co-educational and were presided over by a man and wife, called the superintendent and matron, with equal responsibilities. This was a peculiarly Quaker type of organization; there has been nothing quite like it elsewhere in educational practice. The interdependent life typical of the average Quaker family was closely approximated. Students worked in the garden and on the farm. At Ackworth School in England, which was the prototype of all the Friends' boarding schools, the girls mended the boys' clothes. There was a daily period of family worship, which consisted of a reading from the Bible followed by silence. The school went to meeting together twice on Sunday and once in the middle of the week. Many of the teachers resided in the school building in intimate relation with their pupils. Members of the school committee and Friends traveling with a concern for the ministry were continually coming and going.

These arrangements resulted in a closely integrated community life which exerted a powerful influence on character. This kind of interdependent life is most effective in educating feeling. Thought was thoroughly exercised in the classroom. The Quakers were well aware of the importance of developing the mind and equipping it with the facts, powers, and skills needed for successful living. But they were equally interested in developing that area of the human soul which is deeper than thought, the region into which the Divine Light shines revealing religious and moral truth. This area is not as thoroughly cultivated by specific instruction in the classroom as it is by what might be called a religious and moral atmosphere breathed by young people during all their school days. The impact of the school community on the individual was exclusive. There was no competing influence. The expression "a religious, guarded education," so often appearing in the minutes of Friends meetings, designated the considered effort to keep out distractions. As the student took part in the activities of the school community, he was affected more deeply than would have been possible by studies alone. His feelings were trained as well as his thoughts.

But it must be noted that similar methods can be used to educate evil feelings as well as good ones. The Quakers not only believed in the Inward Light, but they were keenly aware both of inward and outward darkness, a fact which some modern Quakers have decided to overlook. The methods used in their youth organizations by Hitler, Mussolini, and the communists exhibit some aspects of the same pattern. An exclusive community is created. Youth takes part in its closely knit activities which powerfully affect the character and will. But there is this important difference: for the Nazis, fascists, and Russian communists, Truth is relative and subordinate to a particular purpose, while for the Quakers, Truth has always been absolute and independent of human purposes. Man is not the center of the moral universe any more than he is the center of the physical universe. The Quakers do not rely on indoctrination, though they have always firmly believed in expressing Truth as they see it. They believe in exposure to the Light of Truth in the heart, confident that Truth would be apprehended if the right conditions were created to produce a maximum realization of the presence of the Divine Source of Truth within.

This principle is also fundamental to the Quaker business meeting, which arrives at its decisions not by voting but by a search for unanimity, the theory being that, since there is only one absolute Truth, the nearer the meeting comes to that Truth the nearer it will come into unity. Unity, therefore, can be reached if waited for in the right spirit: a humble, genuine searching by the whole group. In this procedure a minimum of power or authority is exercised by any individual or majority.

The same method can be used as an educational technique in those subjects which concern values, but it is not useful in teaching the facts of science or history. The Light Within does not reveal such facts.

It must be recognized that during the age at which young people attend college their reason is at its most intense stage of development. The most important question for them to answer is simply, "Is it reasonable?" Is this particular fact or theory now offered for my evaluation consistent with what I already know? The test of reason is the test of consistency. College students abhor inconsistency. As they grow older they find by experience that life is full of inconsistencies which they are forced to accept, or at least admit. When this stage comes, fortunate are those who know how to resort to the test of feeling in addition to the test of reason. "The heart has reasons which reason knows not of," says the mathematician Pascal, and many inconsistencies are resolved not by reason but by a deeper insight. Job could not reconcile the justice of God with the suffering of the righteous, but he had a religious experience which eventually satisfied him. The college student should be shown that his effort to express all knowledge by a consistent system is not feasible. If religion appears inconsistent with science, it does not follow that one or the other is untrue. There are many inconsistencies within science itself. The recognition of these inconsistencies has often been the means of making way for newer and more profound insights.

If scientific thought gives us one view of life and our religious feelings give us another, we are offered an opportunity for a profound search into the Truth which may be found to include both. When thought and feeling are synthesized, we are on the strongest foundation. This is well illustrated in the case of pacifists faced with conscription—the rational pacifist is in a stronger position, but the man who bases his position both on reason and religion is in the strongest position of all.

The Friends colleges which evolved out of boarding schools or academies kept many of their original characteristics and methods, though they were modified by a large influx of non-Quaker students and staff and by the requirements of standardizing agencies. It is still true that the Quaker colleges, to varying degrees, retain part of the original emphasis on a religiously centered community life which profoundly affects feeling as well as thought. I had never realized this as clearly as when I transferred from teaching in Earlham College to a non-denominational college. This college was characterized by high academic standards and a religiously motivated origin which exerted definite influence on the curriculum, but there was a difference between it and Earlham which is difficult to describe. The Quaker colleges, Guilford, Earlham, and Haverford, in which I have taught (I cannot speak with the same intimate knowledge of the others), possessed a subtle, indefinable quality, a kind of community life centered in the higher values, independent of classroom courses yet not wholly unrelated to them.

It is this which makes a Quaker college distinctive and which, if allowed to develop and grow, will result in implementing the Quaker social testimonies for equality, simplicity, and peace. I shall not elaborate on these social doctrines, but I would like to emphasize one which used to be primary in Quaker thought and experience, but which is now largely overlooked.

The Quakers believed in simplicity or genuineness in speech to a degree which frequently brought them into ridicule. They were opposed to what today would be called "verbalism," the use of words which are not true expressions of what was felt and experienced; words for the sake of words, rather than for the sake of truth. I believe that verbalism is a disease from which our higher education is suffering today. We educate our students in the expert use of speech, an important and useful accomplishment, but as in advertising, this expertness is often used to impress others rather than to express what the speaker really thinks and feels. The forced and rapid reading of innumerable books creates a tendency toward insincerity and indifference in the use of words. William Penn in outlining ten characteristics of a Quaker mentions as one "the use of few words." Modern Quakers would do well to exert greater care in this regard.

One other desirable characteristic may be selected for consideration. If the ideal of a Quaker college as a religiously centered community of students and teachers is to continue to exist, then the college should not be too large. As the college grows, a certain point is reached at which it ceases to be an integrated community and becomes an aggregate of individuals who create small, often competitive, communities within the larger whole. A college created for the purpose here outlined must be small enough for every member to become well acquainted with every other member. When the freshmen have no opportunity to study under the leading teachers on the faculty, the college is too large.

I have pointed out elsewhere that college and university education in our Western culture began by placing the Divine Arts first, the Liberal Arts or the humanities second and the Useful

Arts third. This was the order of precedence of chapel, library and hall—the divine, the human and that which concerned man's relation to nature. In the course of the nineteenth century, the Liberal Arts forged ahead of the Divine Arts and now, in the twentieth century, the Useful Arts, the practical or applied sciences, appear to present the greatest attraction. The Quaker colleges must not lag behind either in the humanities or in science, but perhaps it is given to us in a peculiar way to demonstrate that it is still possible to put the Divine Arts first.

Our Quaker religion, which is based—as is science—on immediate experience, has nothing to fear from the discoveries of science, history, archaeology, or any other honest endeavor of human intellect and reason. It is a frightening fact that many of the most influential teachers today in American colleges and universities are scientific materialists. Those who teach religion and ethics and have religious or moral views of their own, seldom venture to express them fully. Our colleges and universities, especially those under state control, must take no small share of the blame for the prevailing materialistic philosophy in American life. This lays a great responsibility on all religiously centered institutions.

There are only two ways of changing men—one is by education of spirit, mind, and body, and the other is by violence. Quakers are opposed to changes wrought by violence. Such change is superficial and generally creates an inner reaction opposite in direction to the change desired. Education is the one peaceful technique for creating changes for the better. But, as I have endeavored to show, men are not greatly changed by education if education concerns only ideas, theories, and facts, these being on the surface of the mind. We need to extend our education not so much in extent as in depth. We need to reach and to change for the better those deeper feelings which express the inner character of persons. We need to discover and develop methods suited to present conditions for achieving this. Feelings alone give significance and value to life. All else is means rather than meaning, tools by which we move rather than goals to which we go.

Three thousand years ago a Chinese sage named Mohtze believed that men could be educated to do absolutely anything if appropriate methods were used. He observed that the emperor could so educate his soldiers that they would march into a blazing fire if ordered to do so. Mohtze concluded that men could be educated just as effectually to practice universal love and dispense with all strife and contention.

The education of spirit, mind, and body can be a powerful instrument in the hands of a religious group which seeks to bring about the kingdom of righteousness on earth by changing men from within. Quaker methods are based on the belief that in the depths of his soul, man is in contact with the Divine Spirit of Truth and Love. The Seed of Truth was planted when God breathed into man the breath of Life. Our part as teachers is to provide the right soil and nourishment in order that the Seed may grow.

Race Relations
BY
IRA DE A. REID

VI

Race Relations

BY

IRA DE A. REID

Professor of Sociology, Haverford College, formerly, Director of Research, The National Urban League; author: *The Negro Immigrant, In a Minor Key* and co-author of *Sharecroppers All.*

BOTH IN THEIR BREACH and their observance the social relations between peoples of different races and colors may be regarded as the most disturbing and unsatisfactory human relations of our times. The pattern of these relations, tempered at times by political power and prestige or by their noncompetitive character, has been altered within recent years by the world's growing recognition of the worth of individual personality and by its titular acceptance of a political ideal called democracy within which all men, despite their race, creed, color, sex, or place of birth were to be regarded and treated as equals. The western world has known no more revolutionary principle than this one of social and political equality for all men. As propagators have worked for its implementation in the social order they have had to overcome the effects of centuries of acceptance and inaction, during which racial inequality generated its peculiar types of individuals and institutions. Into this situation fits the social movement that we currently label *race relations*. It is an interim movement that seeks to find in the activity of the present some ways for overcoming the inadequacies generated by the past while moving toward the goals indicated for the future.

Dealing as it does with the basic problem of inequality in society, the problem of race relations may be defined as one which arises when men are denied their basic human rights in their personal relations, and when the political policies and practices of society declare and determine that some racial groups are superior to others, and base the services and rewards of the political society upon that superiority. The problem may be further defined as one in which the political principles indicate a support of the theory of equality among all men, but where the practices of that society refute and debase those principles. Within these limits are to be found the major race relations problems of the modern world—the status of Negro peoples in the United States, the political and social status of Asian peoples in the western hemisphere, the position of South African persons of color, and the general position of "mixed bloods" throughout the world. In its widest implications the problem of race relations includes all of the situations comprehended by the International Declaration of Human Rights.

The political world has developed at least four major approaches to the problems of race relations. First, a state or society may refuse to permit any "alien" group to enter its borders save for temporary purposes, or it may decree that only a definite number or proportion of certain peoples may come in during any particular period. This is a method of exclusion that inheres in the present immigration laws of the world's immigrant-receiving nations. It was a basic problem in the resettlement of the world's displaced persons following World War II. Second, a nation or group may ignore or refuse to recognize the degree of nonacceptance being experienced by a racial or color group, believing that, in due course, its principles of equality will prevail without active implementation. This lack of approach is noted throughout the world when one seeks to appraise the situations under which racially mixed populations have arisen. The third approach involves acceptance of the color group but its relegation to a separated or segregated place in the culture. This segregation has come to mean discrimination against the colored group, since in no instance has this separation provided equality of opportunity, treatment, or equipment. The present problem of race relations is especially related to these practices of segregation and discrimination. The final approach is one of assimilation whereby the adjustment of peoples is permitted to take the course that would ordinarily follow culture and race contacts. This is the process that has been followed in the adjustment of peoples of various European stocks. Where this natural process of assimilation has been arrested, a corrective approach, currently described as integration, has been invented. This is one of the current approaches to the adjustment of Negro-white relations in the United States.

In a general way these have been the secular approaches to the problems of race relations in the western world. Where matters of international politics have been involved, the question of race and color have taken on a different complexion from that involving intranational minorities. Thus, the exclusion of Oriental peoples from citizenship in the United States tended to be modified in terms of our experiences with China and Japan in World War II. The problems of race relations arising out of race crossing have in the past been met by setting up new racial boundaries, such as white, colored, and black in the West Indies, or Native, colored, and European in the Union of South Africa.

In the main, the adjustment of mixed-blood peoples is without definition and formulation. As a result, the children born of racially mixed unions in Europe and Asia during World War II and the occupation periods following that event have become the lost people of our generation, there being no acceptable official policy within which to effect a democratic practice. The problems of segregation and discrimination involve the formal and informal practices of the United States where the current efforts are predominantly in favor of their elimination, and the contemporary practices against Asiatics, Africans, and colored peoples in the Union of South Africa where political power seems to rest with those who approve of *apartheid* in some form. Finally, assimilation and integration tend to be self-fulfilling as approaches to the problems of race relations. If racial groups are adjusted and integrated, the problems of race relations do not exist as such, and the evidence for interpreting the problem is lacking. Experience has shown, however, that there is no approach to the solution of race relations that is calculated to cultivate more heat and less light than one which proposes that there shall be no abridgement of any right of any person that is based solely upon his identification in terms of race and color.

It is within this framework of principle and practice that the Quakers have established their approach to race relations and its related aspects.

Friends have had an historic concern for the social problems currently identified as race relations. George Fox and his followers urged Friends to provide religious instruction for their slaves, which many of them did, law to the contrary notwithstanding. As early as 1698 the Philadelphia Monthly Meeting advised that "all masters of families among Friends do Endeavour to bring their negroes to the publick meetings of worship first days." Henry Cadbury reports that regular meetings for Negroes were initiated in Philadelphia by no less a person than William Penn, in support of which he cites the following minute adopted in the monthly meeting for January, 1700:

Our dear Friend and governor, having laid before this meeting a concern that hath lain upon his mind for some time concerning the negroes and Indians that Friends ought to be very careful in discharging a good conscience toward them in all respects, but more especially for the good of their souls; and that they might, as frequent as may be, come to meetings upon First-days; upon consideration whereof this meeting concludes to appoint a meeting for the negroes, to be kept once a month, etc., and that their masters give notice thereof in their own families, and be present with them at the said meetings as frequent as may be.

Such meetings for Negroes seem to have been held for nearly half a century. The last such meeting was held in Fifth month, 1805, "as Friends upon weighty deliberation, were united in the belief that the service of them was over, and they (the blacks) have now several places for worship of their own." By 1840, so diverse were the practices of the several meetings with respect to Negro membership that the London Yearly Meeting of that year both condemned and defended the American Friends. One report charged Friends with "prejudice against people of colour and ill treatment of them and named a case of a Monthly Meeting that sent to the Quarterly Meeting and the Quarterly Meeting sent it on to the Yearly Meeting a proposition to know if a man of colour could be admitted a member of the Society—the Y.M. [Yearly Meeting] decided that he could be admitted."

There can be little doubt that early Friends were of as many minds on the approaches that should be employed in preserving the souls of Negroes and Indians as they were in determining the full weight of their responsibility in abolishing slavery. Minutes of the Philadelphia Yearly Meetings between 1755 and 1758 indicate how mindful the Meeting was of this matter of importing, buying, or keeping slaves. At the Burlington, New Jersey, Meeting in the latter year, John Woolman, "his soul covered with awfulness," weary of the debate and inaction, spoke as follows to his concern:

It is not a time for delay. Should we not be sensible to what He requires of us, and through a respect to the outward interest of some persons, through a regard to some friendships, which do not stand on the inimitable foundation, neglect to do our duty in firmness and constancy, still waiting for some extraordinary means to bring about their freedom—it may be that by Terrible Things in Righteousness God may answer us in this matter.

For more than two hundred years Quakers in the United States have endeavored to find roads of agreement by which they could approach the social problems with which they were concerned. In race relations as in the quest for religious liberty, the cause of peace, the abolition of slavery, temperance, prison reform, care of the mentally ill, service to Indians, and many others, they have sought first to achieve the new social order within the individual, then in the meeting, thereafter to create it in the community where they lived.

Prior to the second decade of this century this responsibility in race relations was seen as one of providing services to Indians on reservations, improving the conditions under which they lived, providing social and educational services for Negroes through the establishment of housing projects, providing scholarship aid programs and programs of social services to Negroes in their separate communities and institutions, and wherever possible serving as members of the operating boards of these institutions. These were unique and needed services, many of them distinctly pioneering in their efforts at social reconstruction; others of them heavily interlaced with the paternalism so typical of the nineteenth century's approach to problems of race and color.

The clue to Quaker approaches in the field of race relations, however, seems to lie in Friends' efforts to develop and maintain a constancy between religious beliefs and social practices. Since this religious belief is basic to all other considerations, there can be nothing other than an identity of religious and social interests. In order to achieve this identity as well as the results desired, said John Woolman in a testimony before the Yorkshire Meeting, Friends must travel four roads—the *Damascus Road* with its "drawings," "concerns," and "awakenings," which leads to the *Jerusalem Road,* a journey requiring conscience and complete commitment to the rightly fashioned life. There follows the *Jericho Road* of action and service in the cause of one's belief. Finally, one travels the *Erasmus Road,* the way of true fellowship with Christians. Whoever rightly travels these roads feels in some degree "that spirit in which our Redeemer gave His life for us."

There can be no doubt that Friends followed these roads in their approaches to abolish slavery in the United States and in their well-known activities in the Underground Railway. Later their concerns were noted in the field of Negro and Indian education. For the period between 1870 and 1919, however, the record of Friends in the problems of Negro-white relations is relatively mute and inglorious. During this period, says one writer, "the fortunes of the Negro minority seem to have faded somewhat into the background. Negro memberships in the Society tended to disappear. Friends often came to share rather uncritically in the prevailing caste system which kept the Negro behind more subtle but no less real barriers than those of slavery." During this same period, however, Quakers made what might be called their most singular and significant contribution to the resolution of the problems of the American Indians. Almost singlehanded they stimulated public and private interest in the problems of the reservations and the nation's responsibilities for effecting a more humane approach to our Indian population.

It would be uncritical indeed to assume that Friends were merely whimsical in their approaches to problems of race and color in human relations. Certainly it is significant that in the latter part of the nineteenth century and the early years of this century the problems of Negro-white adjustment were defined as problems of the South, to be treated somewhat as were foreign missions. Friends were neither particularly strong nor socially active in the South. Furthermore, the period was one in which legislative approaches, more frequently negative than positive, were used to effect the downward adjustment of the former slave populations. Ironically, every guarantee of the Emancipation Proclamation, save legal enslavement as such, was withdrawn from the Negro population of the South during this period. But Friends as a Society have never been particularly prone to act politically. All in all, it was only the continuing, impassioned concerns of individual Friends during this period that kept the approaches of the Society of Friends from becoming more than a matter of historical record.

Those Friends who participated in the work with Indians and Negroes, in the development of educational institutions (pathetically poor though many of these institutions may have been), in the establishment of such organizations as the League on Urban Conditions among Negroes (now the National Urban League), and the National Association for the Advancement of Colored People, and those who gave full years of service in teaching and educational administration—all these, though few in number, were mighty in keeping alive the Quaker teaching that there is "that of God in every man" as an affirmation of the religious and social equality of all men. Without these persons who seemed to live in the real substance of a religion wherein "practice doth harmonize with principle," American Quakerism might well have become known as the religious light that failed race relations during a period of great need.

It was World War I that provided the new stimulus for Quakerism in this field of human relations. Though not until twenty-five years after its establishment did the American Friends Service Committee set up any special work in this area, the beginnings of its concern can be found in the work of Friends who went to Europe in 1919 with gifts of spirit and kind to aid the victims of that holocaust. It was at this time that the problems of human relations achieved a new working definition—they became problems of the peace, a peace that meant not only the absence of war but the building of a truly good society of men as well. With some accuracy one may say that the Society's current interest in race relations began in its approach to the problems of international relations during the period of World War I. The leadership in this approach came not from American Friends, however, but from a recognition of this problem by English Friends.

In 1918 the London Yearly Meeting adopted a statement on the "Foundations of a True Social Order" which said, in part:

The Fatherhood of God, as revealed by Jesus Christ, should lead us towards a Brotherhood which knows no restriction of race, sex, or social class.

This Brotherhood should express itself in a social order which is directed, beyond all material ends, to the growth of personality truly related to God and man.

The opportunity of full development, physical, moral and spiritual, should be assured to every member of the community —man, woman and child. The development of man's full personality should not be hampered by unjust conditions nor crushed by economic pressure. . . .

Similar concerns were expressed by monthly and yearly meetings of American Friends. When we review today's commitments of many Friends' groups and activities of the American Friends Service Committee in the field of race relations, it is difficult to realize that during the ten-year period of intense racial difficulties following World War I, Friends were singularly inactive in the movements designed to eliminate the world-wide restlessness and disaffection among colored populations. The problems of lynchings and race riots in the United States, the problems of Negro migration to the North, the question of discriminatory immigration legislation, the Japanese Exclusion Act, the social problems of colonies (even of India and South Africa), did not fall within the purview of Friends' concerns. It was not until the late twenties that any specific activity in this area became evident. As the emergencies of World War I disappeared, as the needs for European relief and reconstruction became less demanding, and as the world-wide economic depression began to aggravate the position of minorities and majorities as well, the base for newer programs in interracial work was established.

I recall vividly some of those earlier programs. One of the Philadelphia meetings convened a conference on segregation in that city. Friends said that they were interested in working constructively in the field of race relations but found that they were not always of one mind with American Negroes on the question of eliminating segregation. Many Quakers were distressed to learn that Negroes were not unanimous in their opinions on how to approach this formidable problem of American life. This conference was held in the early thirties. As a result of this and succeeding conferences, and after a very successful series of annual institutes on race relations, the two Philadelphia Yearly Meetings were able to adopt a statement on segregation which might be regarded as the basis of current Quaker programs in race relations. This statement was adopted in 1949 after two years of discussion:

A Statement on Segregation

Jesus taught, and exemplified in His life, that love is the highest law and that every individual, of every race and nation, is of supreme worth.

As a religious society which accepts these truths, we are deeply concerned with the patterns of segregation that have developed in our communities, and with the suffering, the waste of talents, the antagonisms, the blocks to spiritual and cultural growth which they involve. We are concerned, too, with what segregation does to members of the dominant group, in making them feel that they are better than others, and developing attitudes verging on contempt, hate, or fear. We are concerned with the experience of children who hear brotherhood preached but see segregation practiced.

In our country today individuals or groups are set off from the main stream of American life on the basis of their religious background, the color of their skin, or the country of their birth. In large ways and small, these people are denied full participation in our community life. They are hampered in buying or renting adequate homes, in securing an education, in opportunities to learn a trade or profession, in finding employment best-suited to their abilities, in using health and hospital facilities, in enjoying recreation and travel. Through all these areas of life they repeatedly experience frustration and humiliation.

We believe that a society motivated by religious and democratic ideals has no place for discrimination such as these. While we are encouraged by signs of a growing practice of integration and inclusiveness in many Friendly institutions, we must face the extent to which segregation still exists in others. If we associate ourselves in natural human relationships with people of all groups, we must welcome them to our meetings and to our communities. We must demonstrate our willingness to work in nonsegregated situations. We must seek to employ members of all groups on their merits. We must work for the establishing of fair employment practices as public policy. Wherever occasion offers, we must practice fellowship by personal example. We must support those in our own membership or outside it who are taking definite steps to carry forward our testimony of friendly living among all human beings.

Even as earlier Friends set themselves to eliminate slavery from their membership, we in our generation set ourselves to overcome the evils of segregation, hoping to enter as they did upon a new and unguessed richness of human fellowship, new and untried deeps of the Divine resources and companionship.

The meaning of this statement for American Quakers may be noted in the various problems with which they have been concerned in recent years. Though not all of the meetings have adopted such statements, the activities of Friends have been moving toward a realization of the principles expressed despite continuing resistances from within and without Friends' groups.

No longer does there seem to be any question about Negro membership in Friends' meetings. In some parts of the South this problem may arise, but generally Negroes may attend or join meetings even in that section of the United States where joint racial participation is against custom if not the law. Though greater acceptance of Quakerism by Negroes and greater acceptance of Negroes by Quaker groups is revealed by this sharing of the silence, the changes that have been effected in other aspects of Friends' interests have not been so pronounced. Some headway has been made in the free acceptance of children of color into Friends' schools and colleges, but there continue to exist schools and colleges that openly or circuitously limit the number of such students. Those schools and colleges that have moved ahead in practicing the equality of their religious testimony have not done so without difficulty. Schools that have not changed their earlier practices have likewise suffered. In general, Quaker schools and colleges are more open to persons of color than ever before. Because of this fact there have arisen the inevitable unanticipated consequences.

The admission of persons of color to Quaker institutions, be they meetings or schools or hospitals, as members or attenders, as teachers or students, as patients or practitioners, raises problems of social contacts. It is in this area of social relations that the "inner piety and outward serviceableness" principle of Friends is having its current test. Should the General Conference of the Religious Society of Friends continue to meet in Cape May, New Jersey, a resort area where racial segregation is the rule? Though the Conference makes special arrangements for the attendance of any Negroes who may come, all of the proceedings take place under this shroud of human indignity. Some Friends questioned whether or not they could conscientiously attend the 1952 General Conference if it were held in Cape May under these conditions. The concern was expressed to the Social Order Committee of the Friends General Conference. The Conference was held as scheduled. It is interesting to note, however, that many national, secular organizations refuse to hold their meetings at any place where their delegates who happen to be colored will experience the hazards of racial segregation. Quakers have not yet achieved that full understanding of the meaning of racial segregation to those who are segregated.

Similarly, the admission of persons of color to our educational institutions, if correct in principle, should lead to effective, friendly human relations despite the differences in skin color or nationality background. A very definite concern within several schools has been expressed over the question of admitting Negro boys, Negro girls, or both sexes. The rationalizations attending the solution of the question are interesting, though all of them may be reduced to the basic problem of cross-race, cross-sex relations. One school, in an effort to regulate the degree to which interracial contacts should prevail across sex lines, limited the number of interracial dates a student might have during a given school period. The academic regulations were established for the "good of the students."

While such a problem may exist within one group of the Society of Friends, another group may be seriously concerned with finding a serviceable way for dealing with the question of interracial marriages. Realizing the necessity for "clearness" in this situation, and recognizing that at least one other Christian group has established both religious and social principles upon which sound and constructive guidance may be given those who seek to unite in such marriages, this Meeting wishes to conserve the sanctity of marriage and family for those who have been denied that privilege by western society. They recognize the feelings, the failings, and the frustrations that are involved in this approach to race relations. They also know that discrimination in the right to marry a person of one's choice is one of the most flagrant discriminations in our society.

The American Friends Service Committee is relatively a newcomer in the field of race relations. As recently as 1944 it formed a committee for this program designed to work closely with the Society of Friends and the various committees of the

Yearly Meetings in the United States. Despite the fact that the program has faced many problems of organization and action, its program has made real contributions to the adjustment of group relations both in the United States and abroad. A detailed analysis of the AFSC work in this field would necessitate description of projects and shared experiences in the fields of professional services in medicine and education, creating equal job opportunities, providing self-help techniques in housing and community development, demonstrating interracial participation by including persons of color in all of the organization's service programs and in various places on its staff and committees. For the Service Committee, race relations has meant service to and with Negroes as well as Indians, Jews and Oriental-Americans. By its own interpretation the Race Relations Program begins to reach around the world. Its contribution toward the large concept of "a healthy, unified mankind" begins to make itself clear. Let us examine this assertion.

1. **The problem:** *Racial and religious barriers in the United States have prevented many white students and teachers in preparatory schools and colleges from becoming acquainted with Negroes of similar intellectual and social attainments. Correction of this deficiency should lead to a sense of togetherness and should provide a strengthened foundation of racial, religious, and social understanding.*

The AFSC approach to this situation was the creation of a program of visiting lecturers and exchange professors. This program made available to American preparatory schools and colleges the services of Negro scholars, well known in their own intellectual fields. Since 1945 these lecturers have conducted classes in their own subjects, have met with informal groups of faculty and students, and for periods of one week or longer have lived the college life on the several campuses and in the wider communities. The program was not only a unique but also a successful venture in race relations. It has provided a new interpretation of race relations for many a Quaker college and a redefinition of the Negro personality for the scores of non-Quaker institutions that have participated in the program. Partly as the result of this effort and experience more than one hundred Negro men and women are now employed on the instructional staffs of institutions whose enrollments are predominantly of white students. Furthermore, lecturers' visits have provided opportunities for conferences on racial and religious problems that were being faced on several campuses. Today the AFSC visiting lectureship program is being introduced to white colleges and universities of the South with a measure of success that could not have been expected ten years ago.

2. **The problem:** *Racial and religious discriminations in employment in the United States have caused a tragic waste of the talents and capabilities of minority peoples. Equality in employment in terms of one's skills and abilities is a basic requirement of the good community. Helping to achieve that equality is a positive act of service and love.*

One of the most active programs in race relations in the United States is that of providing equality of economic opportunity in the fields of employment for minority peoples. Beginning with a program of job placement in 1945, the AFSC proceeded to develop a new approach to the problem of employment on the basis of merit. This program enlisted the resources of the local community, no matter where it was located, in solving for themselves their local problem of minority employment. As the community worked on this problem the Service Committee counseled and shared its experience with management and workers, unions and employer organizations, and community leaders in other fields. The pattern of this co-operation varied from community to community. In Philadelphia it began with the co-operation of other agencies in promoting the Council for Equal Job Opportunities. It continued through the successful campaign to establish a Fair Employment Practices Commission in that city to the final revision of the city charter which called for the establishment of a public-supported Human Relations Commission which now carries forward an enlarged program of employment integration.

In Rapid City, South Dakota, the program is chiefly concerned with the employment of Indians who have moved into the community from nearby reservations. In Greensboro, North

Carolina; Kansas City, Missouri; and Houston, Texas, the problems center around the more useful employment of Negro workers. The AFSC technique in this connection is that of lifting conference and discussion of a social problem from the level of prejudice in the employment of Negroes and Indians to the level of merit employment of human beings. AFSC staff personnel point out that they are not experts telling businessmen how to run and manage their enterprises, but are "concerned, religiously motivated, average people with years of business experience in our own lives." In the year 1950–51 this program worked with 221 businesses on ways of solving the problems of integration as Quakers see them.

3. **The problem:** *Lack of training, occasioned by unequal educational opportunities, frequently limits and prevents discriminated-against people from obtaining and holding more responsible and remunerative positions than those on which they are now employed.*

Changing the employment pattern of a community with respect to its utilization of persons ordinarily discriminated against in jobs is a pioneering venture for the counselor, the employer, and the applicant. The Service Commitee discovered that its program of employment on merit would have deeper significance only if it could find ways for training and encouraging young people in the intricacies of employment pioneering. This consideration led to the establishment of a job applicant training program. This workshop is designed to provide young people with a knowledge both of job trends and employer requirements. Community leaders and organizations provide the sponsorship, sometimes in co-operation with the Service Committee. They also provide meeting rooms, publicity, and discussion leaders.

The usual workshop of six to ten sessions brings to a small group of young people information and help through soundfilms, voice recordings, sociodramas and visual aids. Industry, schools, and local agencies provide the guidance of competent counselors. Particular attention may be given to the problems faced by minority groups, and often for the first time schoolmates feel a new sympathy and understanding when they see the difficulties that ignorance and prejudice place in the paths of their friends. More than all else, the conviction that someone else is really interested in their problems brings a new sense of encouragement to these young people.

4. **The problem:** *Many communities wish to find ways and means for ameliorating or eradicating the heavy burdens of prejudice and discrimination which they bear. Such needs provide significant opportunities for Quakers to speak of their concerns.*

There is no aspect of AFSC's race relations program that has deeper meaning for Quaker approaches than the extent to which the organization is called upon to counsel with local groups and communities on their specific problems. The requests are varied: how to get Negroes on the local police force; how to combat prejudices among minority groups; how to overcome the situations that led to a race riot; what steps to take to secure the employment of a social worker who passed highest in a civil service examination but could not get a job; review of a co-operative, racially integrated housing program in which the financial risks of integration can be borne equally by those living in the project and by members of the co-operative; consideration of a program for training workers to deal with an experimental program for street corner gangs; and advising local communities on ways for improving their human relations.

Two specific examples of AFSC work in community co-operation will illustrate Quaker approaches to the problem at hand.

Between 1940 and 1947 approximately 250,000 Negroes migrated from the South to the defense industry areas of the Pacific West. Some 4,000 of this number went to be employed in the Kaiser shipyards of Richmond, California. Today many of this number are now living in rows of trailers and shacks in a 60-city blocks area of North Richmond. Now that the shipyards are closed, many of the workers are unemployed. Economic and social pressures are intense. After sponsoring several work camps in North Richmond, the AFSC established a Neighborhood House which provides individual aid in family and employment problems, such social activities as might make less distressing the unsatisfactory living conditions. As the

Neighborhood House becomes more of a center for neighborhood activity, the Service Committee will indicate community work on basic problems.

The second approach is a project of urban self-help housing. The site is in an interracial neighborhood of Philadelphia. The houses, which though run-down are structurally sound, are being renovated. Residents of the block are doing work which does not infringe on city codes. All other work is being done by a contractor. The project is sponsored by the AFSC in co-operation with the Friends Neighborhood Guild, the City Planning Commission, the Redevelopment Authority, the City Council of Philadelphia, the Federal Housing Administration, and two Philadelphia banks.

5. **The problem:** *The American Indian has been a concern of Quakers for more than 250 years. As many Indians are now leaving reservations and moving to urban communities, need has arisen for plans to rehabilitate and integrate this population into our national life and to provide immediate material relief for its migrant groups.*

The changing character of American Indian needs has necessitated changing programs. Thus, the usual programs for relieving the inadequacies of reservation life are no longer sufficient to guarantee constructive social gains. Current approaches to this important aspect of race relations in the United States are typified in four ways by the AFSC.

Material needs of Indians on reservations are met through shipments of clothing, establishment of sewing rooms, and the initiation of volunteer work camps. In the work camps non-Indian young people and Indians work side by side on vital Indian community projects such as building school dormitories and constructing community buildings. This type of program has been carried on each summer since 1949.

A newer program attends the movement of Indians from reservations into communities. Since 1948 some 40 Navajo and Hopi children have—through the AFSC's Child Visitation Program—spent two weeks each summer in the Los Angeles area with non-Indian families who have children the same ages. This project is very similar to a program for Negro and white children conducted by non-Quaker agencies in the East and provides excellent opportunities for long-range good will relations between individuals and between family groups.

A major project of the off-reservation Indian program has been an Indian Center conducted since the early 1930's, first by the California Yearly Meeting of the Society of Friends, later by AFSC. It is estimated that there are at least 5,000 Indians in the Los Angeles area, many of whom need help in adjusting to city life both because of the discrimination they encounter and the vast differences between the tempo of city life and that on the reservations from which they have come. The Center provides counseling on problems of employment, housing, and medical services; group activities such as crafts, folk dancing, and religious services; a lounge for leisure time activities and informal meetings; a meeting place available to Indians and Indian-interested organizations; and a center for the dissemination of accurate information on Indians and Indian affairs.

As a result of the experience gained in the Los Angeles area, and in co-operative relations with public and private agencies in Flagstaff, Arizona, the AFSC has gone to Rapid City, South Dakota, where 2,000 Indians seek employment and live in camps on the outskirts of the city in conditions described as worse than those in many city slums. In Rapid City the AFSC, after making a survey of the needs that must be met, recommended the use of a community counselor who would try to help the existing agencies co-ordinate their services to the Indian peoples. This is indeed a pioneering project that will eventually include tried Quaker approaches in the fields of housing, health, education, and employment.

6. The problem: *Race relations are improved when the discriminated-against peoples have opportunities to share as equals in programs designed to bring about unity in mankind.*

Truly effective human relations demand that all persons have an opportunity to give as well as to receive the voluntary services of concerned people. The Quaker approach to human brotherhood includes the services of those who give as well as those who receive. In self-help programs, work camps, internesin-industry, student seminars, work in mental hospitals, and programs of foreign service are to be found persons of all races and creeds working together without segregation, friction, or awkwardness born of awareness of visible though superficial differences. An American Negro physician headed the AFSC medical mission among Arab refugees in southern Palestine; an educator and his wife directed the work of the Friends service unit in India; a college secretary set up the first Austrian work camp and directed the work of rebuilding a town. Teams of young students of all races and creeds work, study, and live together in their efforts to give human brotherhood a real reference in reality.

Developing such a program of mutual participation is not easy. Minority groups, in general, have too little understanding of the deeper significances of Quaker approaches to social problems, of their motivations and concerns. As a result it has been difficult to secure as large a group of Negroes, Indians, and Americans of Chinese and Japanese parentage as the AFSC would desire. This need not be regarded as an insurmountable obstacle when one recalls that Quakers have made little effort to share their religious convictions with persons of other groups, religious or racial, through indoctrination. The acceptance of the principles and the sacrifices involved in *giving* are not learned so easily as are the understandings derived from *receiving*. Though the past decade has brought a truer equality of sharing for Negroes, Indians, and Orientals in Service Committee programs, there remains to be undertaken a basic approach to race relations that would encourage minority peoples to join in the dynamic development of programs that "conscientiously serve humanity."

One needs not be told that the problems of race relations in the modern world can no longer be treated as superficial aspects of human and national relations. Few would doubt that the ways in which we practice human relations with persons of other races, creeds, and nationalities are important factors in determining the nature of the peace under which our world society will survive or wither. As Friends begin their fourth century they well may ponder their vocation from two points of view—the portents of race relations in the modern world, and the tested principles and practices of Friends that may be related to these portents.

Nationality and nationalisms are important factors in the race relations picture. Ironically, the problems of the nations of colored peoples are not decided on the basis of race and color so much as they are on the basis of political expediency. The world has found it easier to deal with the symbols of nation than with the symbol of color and religion. Today the world has an opportunity to face the issues that minority peoples and minority nations present through acting upon and implementing the Declaration of Human Rights. Even if this document becomes a world-wide treaty, we shall be faced with the approach of implementing it in our international behavior. Today Friends are concerned with the race problems of the Union of South Africa. Since 1938 American and British Friends have sought to effect some reconciliation of the differences that have typified the development of this racially divided nation from the early years of the century. *Apartheid* is but a variant of the segregation and discrimination that has typified the acceptance of nonwhite peoples in the western world.

The vocation of Friends seems to call for an approach that will prevent the spread of segregation and discrimination of persons on the basis of color, race, religion or nationality, whether these practices obtain in the Orient or the Occident, in South Africa, India, Europe, Israel, or Southeast Asia. Friends are cautioned to look to these areas and to the West Indies and Latin America for portents that bespeak a developing society of men based on such distinctions.

Beyond these there seem to be two general situations that bespeak Friends' concern. One is the necessity for realizing that the problems of colonies, of trusteeship as it is now known, are the problems of race relations with political and economic overtones. We cannot say that we have created a new climate for human brotherhood until we have found ways for providing bonds of unity with the people of the world who suffer the triple indignities of despised race, impoverished economy, and voiceless politics. Secondly, the world has been creating larger and larger numbers of peoples currently defined as mixed bloods who are being denied rights and privileges in their country of birth but whose plight must be recognized as we reformulate the principles and practices of human brotherhood.

But the vocation of Friends in the modern world does not find expression in foreign fields alone. The United States continues to offer formidable challenges to men and women who respond to the divine call within. As the leading immigration-receiving nation of the world, we shall be called upon to continue our revision of immigration laws until they permit no discrimination on the basis of race, color, or creed.

Friends will be called upon to provide greater evidence of reality for the beliefs they profess. They may well indicate ways by which the discriminated persons of the world and those who profess belief in the equality of men might live beyond the secular laws that segregate and discriminate against Negroes and Indians and persons of Oriental ancestry.

Friends will be called upon to come out of their meetings and visit the South as they have visited South Africa and India and Russia, noting the conditions with which they must deal as lovers and promoters of peace.

But why say that Friends are called upon to pursue such courses? Only because the world believes that members of the Religious Society of Friends are peculiarly endowed with an ability to understand and deal with the material and spiritual needs of man. Friends themselves may know better, but the world believes that they do not truckle to the political or social expediency of the moment. It is to be hoped that the nations and peoples of the world will continue to so believe, for there inheres in the principles and practices of Friends' religion the power to spur people onward "not into deadening repetitions" but into new and positive acts of service and love. This belief seems to exact of Quakers that they continue to promote the methods of agreement through which so much has been achieved; that they recognize the welcome with which men receive the techniques of nonviolence as ways by which the world may achieve true brotherhood; that they recognize the increasing importance of legislation in determining the conditions of human adjustment, and that their activities neither begin nor stop with lobbying for or against legislation but that they interpret active world and national citizenship as an essential practice in the achievement of world-wide brotherhood; that they continue to channel their joy in God into practical patterns by recognizing no limits in human relations beyond which a Friend cannot follow the path of action, no concern that must end with prophesy.

In reviewing their practices and approaches in the field of human brotherhood Friends may continue to be challenged by the two-hundred-year-old consideration of John Woolman—"Whoever rightly advocates the Cause of some, thereby promotes the good of all."

Civil Liberties
BY
HARROP A. FREEMAN

VII

Civil Liberties

BY

HARROP A. FREEMAN

Professor of Law, Cornell Law School, Lecturer in International Affairs and Law, author: *Coercion of States in International Organizations, Peace in the Victory,* and others.

IT IS NEVER EASY to characterize the attitudes, beliefs or activities of a large and heterogeneous group of people. This is particularly true of the Religious Society of Friends which spans three hundred years, most nations, varying levels of education, and all of the economic and social classes. This chapter will, therefore, have to attempt some evaluation of the relation of Quakers to civil liberties and at the same time try to distinguish various currents within the society itself.

It is a simple fact of history that Quakers have established some of the foundation principles of liberty under law, from the time when William Penn's case established the principle that the verdict of a jury cannot be overridden by the judge. Friends have, from the outset, challenged the state in the state's assertion of its supremacy over the individual conscience as in their refusal to doff hats or pay war taxes, and by the "underground railroad," by draft nonregistrants and conscientious objectors. The United States Supreme Court has referred to this as a cause of the recognition of civil liberties. Nor can we deny that formal organizations to protect civil liberties in England and the United States have been strongly supported by Quakers and that the present executive director of the American Civil Liberties Union is a Friend. Throughout its history the Society has defined its position much as did the Five Years Meeting of Friends in 1945:

We affirm our unchanging conviction that our first allegiance is to God, and if this conflicts with any compulsion of the State, we serve our country best by remaining true to our higher loyalty.

This bears a marked similarity to the words of the Supreme Court in *Girouard v. United States*, 328 U.S. 61, 68; decided a few months later:

The victory for freedom of thought recorded in our Bill of Rights recognizes that in the domain of conscience there is a moral power higher than the State. Throughout the ages, men have suffered death rather than subordinate their allegiance to God to the authority of the State.

And this can be echoed in the law writings of Blackstone, contemporaneous with the founding of Quakerism:

No laws are binding on the individual subject that assault his person or violate the conscience.

A brief review of the genesis of civil liberties and of the beginnings of the Religious Society of Friends will show some interesting parallels and perhaps help to demonstrate why Quakers have always been in the forefront in the advancement of civil liberties. It is frequently recognized that institutions developing in the same social milieu almost invariably reflect in varying degrees the same basic assumptions.

There is a direct descent which lawyers trace from the Stoic philosophy and Christian concept of divinely created, free and rational souls, through the martyr conscience of early Christians, through Roman *Jus Gentium* or law common to all peoples, through natural law which posits a law of God written into the universe and governing men's interrelations as the laws of gravitation govern the heavenly bodies and to which national law must conform, to the codified and protected civil rights.

Though the natural law doctrine is today in legal disrepute and is largely being replaced by a sociological or integrated jurisprudence, much of the flavor of the old theory remains and a large segment of legal thought maintains that these new theories are but a new attempt to compare *Is* law (enacted or man made law) with *Ought* law (correct, Divine or natural law). And few there are but recognize that without some concept of *oughtness* and with pure emphasis on *is,* you achieve the totalitarianism of Louis XIV ("I am the law") or of a Hitler.

It is generally recognized that the outstanding English-European dates in the development of civil liberties are: Magna Carta (1215), Statutes of Westminster (1275), treaty of Augsburg (1555), edict of Nantes (1598), Petition of Right (1628), Agreement of the People of England—Puritan Revolution (1647), Bushell's case (1670), Habeas Corpus Act (1679), Bill of Rights (1688), Toleration act (1689), Acts of Settlement (1700-01). In America the dates are: Maryland Toleration act (1649), Charter of Rhode Island (1662), Zenger case (1734), Declaration of Rights and Liberties (1774), Virginia Declaration of Rights and Declaration of Independence (1776), Virginia Statute of religious freedom (1785), Ordinance of the Northwest Territory (1787), first ten amendments to the federal constitution (1791).

Since the Quaker movement started in England about 1640 and in America about 1660, it can be seen that they were in the very vortex of the stirrings which found expression in civil rights. Theirs was a religious expression against authoritarianism and in favor of the individual, against wealth and power and on the side of simplicity, against intrigue, and for truth. The Quaker business meeting, the general lines of which were laid down during this period, carried the religious implication into the field of practical governance of a body. It is perhaps the most democratic government ever devised, outranking the New England town meeting which grew out of the same era. In it there is found full discussion with no vote splitting minority and majority. There is persistent consideration toward an attempted understanding until the "sense" of the meeting is found, willingness to reconsider even after decision, united effort in the decided course, allowance of variation in individual conscience. In these religious insights and patterns of government will be found recognition of most of the reasons which have been given for society guaranteeing civil liberties (as summarized in the *Encyclopedia Britannica*):

1. Natural rights
2. Means of progress (through) ... innovations ... and wiser criticism
3. Self-correction through discussion
4. Recruiting ... potential leadership
5. Safeguarding majority rights
6. Democratic responsibility
7. Peace and loyalty (to that which you can change peaceably)
8. Safety valve
9. Sublimation ... for the common good
10. Public confidence
11. Injustice of repression
12. Avoidance of incitation
13. Futility of repression
14. Fallibility of repression. ...

It is worth while to press the parallel one step further. As we have seen, civil liberties derived from Stoic philosophy, Christian doctrine, and natural law. This reliance on God and universal law gave the needed authority to those who challenged the absolutism of the day. It was the province of national law to find out and declare natural law. Insofar as it accomplished this it was to be obeyed; where it failed, it was to be disregarded. The freedom and rights possessed by men thus to challenge laws were natural or civil liberties and their protection natural or civil rights. Quakers operated much in this tradition. Their central thesis was that there was something of God in every human being, that each in silent communion with God could discover what was in keeping with God's will, that having found this will it must be followed unhesitatingly, that no harm or violation of the personality should be visited on another for in him God had his habitation, and that every effort must be made to preserve to others the right to follow God's leading as they saw it.

Granted that Quakers have a tradition in civil liberties, what are they doing now? We ought to be hesitant to glory in past acts and quick to recognize that too often Quakers live today on the legacies of respect left by the rebels of yesteryear rather than to dare to speak out on modern equivalents of problems which landed their ancestors in prison. The Quaker poet Whittier has well stated this:

> Too cheaply truths once purchased dear
> Are made our own.
> Too long the world has smiled to hear
> Our boast of full corn in the ear
> By others sown.

• What, for example, would be the modern equivalent of refusal to take oaths of conformity? Would it be found in the Baltimore headline describing the refusal of two Quaker ladies to take the Maryland anticommunist oath, not because they were communist but because they opposed witch hunts and oaths: TOLL OF THE OBER LAW—No COMMUNISTS, TWO QUAKERS. We humbly recognize that it has been the Jehovah's Witnesses—not the Quakers—who have again and again taken the cases to the United States Supreme Court which have established principles of religious freedom and free speech in the past thirty years.

More recently the Religious Society of Friends has taken on new significance in the preservation of civil liberties. This is, in part, explainable by the way in which the modern problems originate. The champions of civil liberties are often forced to the fore by events. Thus business in establishing concepts of due process, labor in asserting the right to strike and picket, Negroes in defending themselves in criminal cases, Jehovah's Witnesses faced with city and state laws against meetings and pamphlet distribution, have all developed principles of civil liberties for others, which perhaps none but they could have done. Quakers likewise may now be at a critical hour.

It is recognized that in the past few years the Supreme Court has struck down frequently state and local action interfering with civil liberties—unequal segregation, all-white juries, coerced confessions, restrictions of newspaper comment on trials, requirement of permits to distribute pamphlets or address meetings, compulsory flag salutes, failure to give police protection, censorship of movie or newssheet. So it can be said that as never before civil liberties are safe against local and state interference. But, and it is a large *but,* are they safe from federal interference? Not in about fifteen years has the Supreme Court (with the exception of the recent steel seizure decision) held invalid federal action as interfering with civil rights. In that period, federal removal of the entire Japanese-American population from the West Coast into concentration camps, loyalty processing and immigration refusals without the rudiments of a fair hearing, procedures of Un-American Activities Committees, peacetime conscription, government seizure of plants and government breaking of strikes, guilt by association, federal definition of religion, prevention of advocacy without incitement, and other action previously thought to be contrary to recognized principles of civil liberties have received open or tacit Court approval.

All these suppressions of civil liberties by the federal government are performed in the name of a higher value—the self preservation of the nation-state. In short, under (a) the war power or (b) the power to suppress violent revolution against the nation, individual freedom is fast disappearing. Granted that the nation (the people as a whole) has the right of self-preservation and that no country can be expected to guarantee to anyone the right to overthrow it violently, we must recognize that for the past thirteen years we have been in war or cold war and that communist ideology will continue in the world for years to come; we must either find an area of liberty against the national government at war or recognize that civil liberties are a dead issue.

Precisely because Quaker testimony has always been against war and plottings and one of friendliness and nonviolence, Quakers will have occasion more frequently than others to challenge the government in its use of war powers and cannot be reasonably charged with being advocates or part of a revolution of violence. The most famous statement of Friends, that of

George Fox and eleven others in 1660, is well recognized as the position of the Society:

> The Spirit of Christ, by which we are guided, is not changeable, so as once to command us from a thing of evil, and again to move us to it, and we certainly know and do testify to the world that the Spirit of Christ, which leads us into all truths, will never move us to fight and war against any man with outward weapons, neither for the Kingdom of Christ nor for the kingdoms of this world.
>
> This we can say to the world, we have wronged no man, we have used no force nor violence against any man: we have been found in no plots, nor guilty of sedition. When we have been wronged, we have not made resistance against authority; but whenever we could not obey for conscience sake, we have suffered the most of any people in the nation.

Therefore, when Caroline Foulke Urie refuses to pay taxes for war, the newspapers largely do understand why an eighty-year-old Quaker takes this stand—it is not just a part of the general revolt against high taxes. When Dr. Brailie and Doris Schamleffer refuse to take the Ober oath in Maryland, they are recognized as devoted public servants and Quakers rather than Communists. When the Friends Committee on National Legislation testifies against the Mundt-Nixon or McCarran laws, they are understood as protecting civil liberties, not as un-American. And occasionally a nonregistrant Quaker can make a judge "feel like Pontius Pilate."

As one who has been associated with most of these Quaker challenges in the past few years, I can report that virtually none of this action has been motivated by a recognition of the tactically advantageous point at which Quakers find themselves, but humbly, after profound heart searching, relying upon God's leading and with a sense of the awfulness of the hour. And they have suffered with the strength of meekness. Never shall I forget Larry Gara, college dean of men who served a second term in prison for telling a young nonregistrant that he stood with him; Steve Simon and many others who have served two and three terms under the cat-and-mouse procedure though their offense was really single, the refusal to co-operate with the war system. But above all I recollect the quiet courage of Robert Michener and his bride. The young man was only nineteen and possessed of a legal defense that might have saved him, but when he was pushed by a United States attorney and given the most severe sentence the law would allow, he quietly faced a fifteen-year second sentence for refusal to be inducted, although it was conceded he was a C.O. and should not be inducted. On such foundations are civil liberties builded.

It has become the accepted pattern in writing about Civil Liberties to dwell in detail on the Bill of Rights and the civil rights thereby guaranteed:

1. Freedom of religion, press, speech, assembly, and petition
2. Right to bear arms and be free of quartered soldiers
3. Right to trial by jury and freedom from unreasonable search and seizure
4. Life, liberty, and property not to be taken without due process of law
5. Freedom from double jeopardy, excessive bail or fine, and from cruel and unusual punishment

Those rights dealing with protections for men charged with crimes have been well defined and asserted until, with all its faults, the federal criminal system is recognized as one of the most humane in the world. Conscientious objectors are continuing to aid in its improvement by their hunger strikes against Negro segregation, use of the "hole" and similar practices. Freedom of religion has in many respects gained marked protection, the right to distribute literature, to preach, to play phonographs on the street or from house to house without a permit or license tax, the right to refuse to salute the flag. The position of Negroes has greatly improved through decisions prohibiting segregation in interstate travel, more rigid tests of equality, nonenforcement of restrictive covenants. Much greater freedom of speech and press has come into being in the Hartzell, Taylor, Bridges, Terminiello, and similar cases.

It is not of these I would speak, but rather of four areas in which civil liberties issues are acute and where it is fairly clear that Friends will play a significant part. These are:

1. Conscientious objection to war and war preparation
2. Loyalty oaths and programs
3. Legislative investigations of un-Americanism
4. New civil liberties represented by such expressions as the International Bill of Human Rights and the right to economic security

At no point has the Society of Friends more openly and consistently challenged the nation's interference with individual liberty than in conscientious objection to war service and all contributions to the war effort. And this area also most adequately illustrates the closeness of the relationship of Friends' religious theory and the position on civil liberties. This opposition has taken the form of refusal of military service, service in Civilian Public Service Camps and hundreds of mental hospitals and other alternative programs, nonregistration or refusal to report for Selective Service induction, counseling others to follow conscience and refuse to register, work strikes, refusal to pay taxes or participate in fire watching or "civil defense." The record in England during the war can be found in Denis Hayes', *Challenge of Conscience* and in America in the releases from the Central Committee for Conscientious Objectors in Philadelphia or the book by Jacobs and Sibley, *Conscientious Objectors in Warld War II.*

Particularly since the war, Quakers have been the most numerous nonregistrants. A called meeting of the Society in 1948, after quoting Fox's declaration of 1660, strongly commended civil disobedience—and this has subsequently been reaffirmed numerous times:

Friends are exhorted to adhere faithfully to this testimony against all wars and fighting, and in no way to unite with any warlike measure such as a Selective Service Draft or Universal Military Training, to the end that we may convincingly demonstrate a more excellent way of settling conflicts. . . . A living concern having been expressed that Friends' practices be consistent with their professions, Friends are urged:
 1. To support Young Friends and others who express their opposition to conscription either by nonregistration, or by registration as conscientious objectors. We warmly approve civil dis-

obedience under Divine compulsion as an honorable testimony fully in keeping with the history and practices of Friends. [Here follow other recommendations, e.g., considering nonpayment of war taxes, nonparticipation in war work, defense bond purchases, etc.]

Quakers consistently maintain that pacifism and obligation to abide by the laws of God rather than the laws of man are religious necessities illustrated throughout the Bible and Christian history and that a correct appraisal of the adoption of our constitution and its amendments shows that the right of conscientious objection is a constitutional right which cannot be taken away by Congress. In this latter regard Friends take a stronger position than most civil liberties advocates and lawyers, who tend to consider conscientious objection not as a constitutional right but as a statutory grace. The United States Supreme Court has referred to freedom of conscience in both ways; they have avoided a clear-cut decision.

The argument of Quakers runs somewhat as follows: The Old and New Testaments show that Judeo-Christian religion has always maintained and practiced duty to the law of God as paramount to duty to man-made law. The first three chapters of Genesis allegorically tell what happens when man violates the will of God; in the first two chapters of Exodus, Moses' parents are commended for breaking the law by fleeing with him to Egypt. The breaches of law by Jesus are well known: teaching and healing on the Sabbath, plucking and eating corn, not washing hands. Two of the first acts of the disciples were breaches of law, producing the arrest of Peter, John, and Stephen, and resulting in Peter's words, "Whether it be right in the sight of God to harken unto you more than unto God, judge ye." This is the unbroken line of religious, and for that matter, of much legal, teaching down through history. It is equally clear that pacifism—the substitution of love, even of enemies, for violence—is the center of Christianity. Historians and theologians recognize that for the first three centuries the Christian church was completely pacifist and martyrs died by the thousands for refusal to war or even to render a "pinch of incense" to Caesar.

Quakers believe they are an example of the continuity of this central Christian theme. Certainly the framers of the Declaration of Independence and the Constitution knew of this position of Quakers who had been the governors and legislators of many of the colonies since their position was referred to by Washington and others in the writings of the day. When, therefore, the Declaration of Independence stated that men "are endowed by their Creator, with certain inalienable rights. . . . That to secure these rights, governments are instituted among men," and then went on to institute a government, is it not a fair conclusion that conscientious objection was protected as an "inalienable" or "constitutional" right? The history of ratification and amendment of the Constitution makes this position even more clear.

As the states ratified the Constitution, nearly every one demanded certain amendments including religious freedom and freedom of conscience. For example, the New Hampshire request was for an amendment: "Congress shall make no laws touching religion or to infringe the rights of conscience." Madison, accordingly, introduced the first proposed amendment to the Constitution on June 8, 1789: ". . . the civil rights of none shall be abridged on account of religious belief or worship, nor shall any national religion be established, nor shall the full and equal rights of conscience be in any manner, or on any pretext, infringed." The substance of this amendment was approved and finally as a clarification of wording, but not as a denial that religious freedom embraced freedom of conscience, the present language was adopted: "Congress shall make no law respecting an establishment of religion, or prohibiting the free exercise thereof."

When the amendment guaranteeing to the people the right to keep arms was proposed, it contained a clause stating that "no person religiously scrupulous shall be compelled to bear arms." In the course of debate the whole history of conscientious objection by Quakers and others was reviewed and marked for protection, but was deemed protected without any such specific clause. All but one of the thirteen original states contained protection of conscience as a part of religious freedom. Pennsylvania's provision may be cited: "All men have a natural and indefeasible right to worship Almighty God according to the dictates of their own consciences; . . . no human authority can, in any case whatever, control or interfere with the rights of conscience."

Quakers regard as a step toward the recognition of their contention, since it cites the acts of Quakers, and as a charter of freedom, the ringing words of the Supreme Court in *West Virginia v. Barnette* (second flag salute case) and propose to maintain this charter even against a reactionary court:

. . . freedom to differ is not limited to things that do not matter much. That would be a mere shadow of freedom. The test of its substance is the right to differ as to things that touch the heart of the existing order.

If there is any fixed star in our constitutional constellation, it is that no official, high or petty, can prescribe what shall be orthodox in politics, nationalism, religion, or other matters of opinion or force citizens to confess by word or act their faith therein. If there are any circumstances which permit an exception, they do not now occur to us.

We have illustrated sufficiently at other points of this chapter cases of Quakers who have suffered for their faith. They have received maximum sentences; they have been prosecuted again and again under a cat-and-mouse technique; they have been vilified by judges; they have been browbeaten by boards; they have been denied fair hearings. Judges have tried to force them to plead "guilty" or have tried by persuasion to induce them to give up their faith. Yet, through it all, these young men have maintained their spirit and have presented their cases so effectively that the public has been treated to sermons on the way of love and jurymen have again and again told us, "You are right though the judge made us find him guilty." Inexorably there is being written such a black page in American protection of civil liberties that a way out must be found—as it was with Negroes and criminals and Jehovah's Witnesses.

We have had in both nation and state a perfect rash of "loyalty" investigations. The Taft-Hartley Act requires affidavits of noncommunist affiliation before a union can utilize the labor law procedures set up; the President's Loyalty Order of March 21, 1947, requires a finding of loyalty or disloyalty for some 2,500,000 federal employees under a test to discover if "reasonable grounds exist for the belief that the person involved is disloyal." State and federal laws have demanded affidavits of loyalty and noncommunist affiliation of teachers and public employees. Just as I was writing the preceding paragraph I was visited by an F.B.I. agent checking on the loyalty of a Quaker job applicant.

These programs, which have all been upheld by courts, pose a problem not usually faced in civil liberties matters. The Supreme Court upheld the Taft-Hartley provision on the ground that remedial legislation could lay down the conditions under which one could gain its advantages, that no man had a right to the law's advantages. So also a government employee is said not to have a right to his job and to be subject to removal for various reasons satisfactory to the executive; but if one of these is communist sympathy or "disloyalty," the courts cannot protect the worker. Treason or "disloyalty" has always been considered a serious crime. We have always maintained in this nation that a person is presumed innocent until proven guilty, is entitled to confront and disprove his accusers. It was assumed in *Lovett v. U.S.* that to prevent a person from retaining his job with the federal government was "punishment," sufficiently criminal in nature so as to bring into being all these subsidiary civil liberties protections. But the courts have held, over vigorous dissents, that these well-known rules do not apply. Though the end result of the federal investigation in terms of employee clearance may be good, the by-products in fear, discouragement from employment of the highest type of people, use of the most outlandish gossip, and such tests as reading the *New Republic* or reports of the *Consumers Union* are not worth the candle.

I have referred elsewhere in this paper to members of the Society of Friends who have openly challenged the Loyalty Oath statutes. Every month brings evidence of new cases. In the past week I read the story of a Pennsylvania woman who had taught beyond the age of retirement in unstinting service and then refused to take the loyalty oath and thereby sacrificed one-half of her pension. These cases sing a great refrain: the free soul cannot be bought.

I have intentionally referred to legislative committees and not merely to the House Un-American Activities Committee because on the crest of hysteria many states and even cities have set up similar committees. And I have described their investigations as prescribing Americanism rather than investigating activities, as they were supposed to, for few have paid any real attention to activities but instead have concentrated on fixing what is orthodox in belief and on attacking individuals for their beliefs and associations rather than acts.

There are many things to protect civil liberties that Quakers can and will continue to do. They have continued to allow to participate in foreign affairs conferences some of those attacked but not proven guilty. They have not withdrawn their support from liberal organizations such as branches of the A.C.L.U., when they have been branded as subversive. They have opposed the creation and continuance of the committees and their methods. They have publicized committee methods, challenged committee procedure and labels, insisted on the presumption of innocence of those attacked until proven guilty, and endeavored to hold down hysteria whenever possible. These are exactly the slow, painstaking procedures which will remove the legislative investigation from its present position as a blot on our civil liberties record. The task will be long, the victory will not come tomorrow; but already the excesses of the committees and the quiet dignity with which they have been opposed presages an improvement in civil liberties protections.

Civil liberties are related not merely to the past or to local issues; they pertain to and take on meaning from future trends and international occurrences. When the recent constitutions adopted throughout the world are examined, it is impressive that nearly every one, in addition to the rights of freedom of speech, press, religion, assembly, contain variously expressed new freedoms, often economic. Thus, they establish right to employment, to minimum standards of living, union activity, collective bargaining, participation in management, health, leisure, equal access to education. The United States, which contains no similar constitutional provision, has incorporated in the Japanese Constitution the right "to maintain the minimum standards of wholesome and cultural living" and the right to work, organize, bargain, and act collectively (Arts. 25, 27, 28). Similar provisions occur in the German constitutions, in the Nationalist and Communist Chinese, in the South American, Near-East, and European. Even here in America we have added to the original protectionist view of civil liberties a reformist view—or as Edward S. Corwin puts it in *Liberty Against Government:*

Basically such claims are of two types: first, *the claim that government protect the claimant in the safe continuance of his existing way of life;* second, *the claim that government contribute something to the improvement of the claimant's way of life.*

President Roosevelt in his message to Congress of January 11, 1944, and his Chicago speech of October 28th, gave voice to this same reformist concept.

The International Bill of Human Rights embodies much the same idea, and there was strong pressure from other sources to get America to approve inclusion of even more of these reformist rights compared to the old, political, civil liberties. The latest letter from the Friends Committee on National Legislation tells of a bill in Congress that would prevent adoption of the international charter, of the Committee's opposition to the bill, and asks Quakers to prevent its passage and work for the adoption of the international rights. Friends have also been asked to draft certain provisions of the International Bill and have done so. Although the courts have continued to reject the argument, Friends and like-minded people continue to urge international concepts of civil liberties as authority for their refusal to participate in war or to pay war taxes and for opposition to restrictive covenants and like inequalities. A Canadian court has deemed a restrictive covenant violative of the United Nations charter and recently a conscientious objector lawyer has submitted a petition to the United Nations Assembly to declare whether international civil rights and U.N. principles justify him in refusing to pay taxes or otherwise participate in America's war and preparation-for-war effort.

By no means have all Quakers accepted the reformist concept of civil liberties—and this issue is closely related to the danger from anarchism, next to be discussed. Yet it cannot be denied that Friends' basic theory of "that of God in every man" predisposes them to a classless society. Any questioning of the reformist theory is not so much with the end sought as with the method employed. The great increase in government and taxes may well persuade us against immediate fulfillment of some of these rights, but they cannot turn us from their ultimate propriety.

Quakers are, perhaps, able to illustrate the most difficult problem of liberty—and for that matter, of democracy itself. It is a problem which has never been satisfactorily solved, the balance between liberty and license, between opposition to government and anarchy.

Democracy is based upon majority responsibility for government and minority criticism and opposition. The majority represents a status which it attempts to maintain and of which it guarantees the stability without which government and peoples cannot be secure. The minority seeks recognition of new rights and change, without which government and peoples cannot grow. Out of new alignments of minorities grow new majorities. Society arrives at a new and more inclusive status. Such society is dynamic; such society has a purpose. A vocal minority is as essential to a democracy as a responsible majority. There is always a "lunatic fringe" that tempts the majority to suppress the minority, for its attacks are bitter and often untrue. But since any idea contrary to accepted mores seems folly, it is hard objectively to separate future wisdom from nonsense. Society must, therefore, tolerate the crackpot or doom itself to stagnation. Our courts have often stated the high ideal of open competition of ideas in the marketplace and the faith that in such encounters truth will win out.

But new techniques of propaganda, the apparent contradiction of this faith in totalitarian countries, and the firm conviction of super-patriots that the country's problems cannot be left to the slow procedures of democratic debate have branded all opposition to government as bad. And such position becomes easy to sell when the minority can be correctly or incorrectly described as giving aid and comfort to the country's enemies. The principle is clear enough—the need to maintain the right of opposition to government occurs, anarchy results. Government ceases. The fine line between open criticism or opposition to government and anarchy or violent revolution is not easy to maintain. This fear of open opposition to government compared to the undercover criminal can well be illustrated by a report of the Central Committee for Conscientious Objectors which has been widely quoted:

Whenever a conscientious objector engages in conscientious disobedience of the Selective Service Act, he commits what the courts regard as a very serious offense. The everyday run of criminal cases involves evaders; persons who have violated law secretly but who have been unsuccessful in "getting away with it." The courts are familiar with this, and, in imposing a penalty in such a case, often feel that lenient treatment will be sufficient to bring the evader back into line. Thus 38.8% of those convicted of serious offenses in the United States courts in 1946-7 were given probation or suspended sentences, and the percentage is much higher in some Federal districts (i.e., New Hampshire, 88%; Massachusetts, 72%).

But a C.O. who has openly violated a law because he cannot in conscience obey it, and who by his very action is claiming a superior allegiance to some "higher" law, is regarded by most judges in a very different light. In case after case one finds judges and U.S. attorneys using the word "defiance" to characterize these young men who stubbornly insist that they are "above the law." Frequently the government points out that the freely elected representatives of the people in Congress have passed this law; that the objector should abide by this majority decision instead of pitting "his puny weight against the will of the Congress"; that if every one violated "any law he didn't like" chaos and disorder would result. That the conscientious objector may be "sincere," "high-minded," etc., is often admitted, but in "taking the law into his own hands," he is felt by the judges to be threatening the whole framework of law and order upon which the republic rests. Viewed in this light, it is entirely logical that the average sentence for conscientious objection in World War II was greater than that for narcotics or white slave violations, and that out-and-out evaders received more lenient treatment than those who justified their disobedience by an appeal to conscience.

It is by making this appeal to "higher law" that conscientious law-violators so inflame opposition to themselves in the courts. Instead of penitently bending to the will of law and majority they seem to be saying, "I am right and everyone else is wrong." Yet such justification for law-breaking, and the hostility it evokes among the guardians of law and order, form one of the most persistent, tragic, yet inspiring threads in the fabric of world history.

Closely related to this problem is the distinction between liberty and libertine. Courts have stated again and again that my liberty ends where another man's nose begins and that no man is at liberty to shout "Fire!" in a crowded theater. The liberty of one presupposes the control of the liberty of others. Liberty is a condition in society and not in a vacuum. In working their way out of this problem the courts have tried to accommodate society's interests to those of the individual by gradually developing the doctrine of "clear and present danger"— that is, that a man will be protected in his freedom of speech or religion or other civil liberty up to the point where it presents a clear and present danger to cardinal interests of society.

Here, again, the principle is clear enough but its application extremely difficult. There is little logical basis for a Supreme Court to decide that Jehovah's Witnesses can play victrola records attacking Catholics in the Catholic section of Boston and create a potential riot (*Cantwell v. Massachusetts*) without creating a clear and present danger, but that a conscientious objector father cannot in the privacy of his own home discuss with his son nonregistration for the draft (*U.S. v. Warren;* the son in fact chose to register), particularly in the light of the clear statement by the Court:

What finally emerges from the "clear and present danger" cases is a working principle that the substantive evil must be extremely serious and the degree of imminence extremely high before utterances can be punished. [*Bridges v. California,* 314 U.S. 252, 263.]

Hidden in every champion of civil liberties is something of the hermit, something of the desire to be left alone. It is no accident that the author of the Declaration of Independence and many of our great civil liberties documents, Thomas Jefferson, believed that the least government was the best government. Most of us recognize the demands of society, but we are also constitutional anarchists at heart. And particularly is this true of a people like the Society of Friends which seeks its religious experience not in song and organ, not in pomp and pageantry, but in silent meditation in small groups. It is, therefore, not strange to find many Quakers who support "rugged individualism," who oppose OPA and rent control, who deplore the great growth in bureaucracy. It is a temptation to move over from opposition to government, because it infringes on the very essentials of human life to oppose government, per se. Many members of the Society of Friends are aware of this dilemma.

In passing, we might mention a position of many Quakers which is often cited—unjustifiably—as showing that they are really anarchists and that their civil liberties position is also unsound. That is the opposition of many or most Friends to punitive criminal law, to armed police, and particularly to an international army. Their critics assume that "law and order" necessarily means "coercive" law and order and that to oppose coercion is to oppose law. Nothing could be farther from the truth. Jurisprudence has always recognized that just and appropriate laws will be obeyed without coercion and that no amount of coercion can or should be able to impose an unjust law continuously.

Friends are in that great tradition that urges that our criminal laws be made truly just and for the rehabilitation of men rather than for vindication, and that our international order be fair and mutually beneficial rather than a struggle of power

K

and advantage, and that as we approach these goals the feeling of need for coercion will die. Because of their peculiar interest in love rather than violence, Friends need to continue their contribution to political thought. Further, in this day when fear of communism as a doctrine that advocates the violent overthrow of government by force tends to label all opposition to government as violent revolution, Quakers with their long history of nonviolence are well able to maintain government criticism on a nonviolent basis.

Crime and Punishment
BY
CURTIS BOK

VIII

Crime and Punishment

BY

CURTIS BOK

Presiding Judge of the Court of Common Pleas No. 6, Philadelphia. Author: *I Too, Nicodemus, The Backbone of the Herring.*

THE PRISON SYSTEM is rooted essentially in revenge, and it always has been.

Those who misbehave must be punished, and we begin practicing this belief on our children long before we get around to dealing with breakers of the criminal law. Most parents refuse to believe that their sons, after an infraction of the rules at home, will be better boys if locked up in the cellar for thirty days with a selection of hoodlums from the vicinage, but if they are honest, they will admit to a slight sadistic thrill when they inflict punishment. It is an easy contagion of the human spirit to trade hurt for hurt, and we grow up to consider punishment as the proper currency in which a criminal should pay his debt to society.

It was much worse at one time, when criminal sanctions were limited to death and torture, with or without exile. It was a Quaker conception, at least in America, to substitute imprisonment for these older forms of punishment. Since this was begun with substituting solitary confinement that was truly solitary and hard labor that was really hard, we feel that we have made progress because we have abolished both solitary confinement and labor, whether hard or easy. Some ameliorations have been added: a general menu in place of bread and water, radios, some prison shops, and libraries of restricted range. Now and then a few devoted souls, recalling their Bible, visit the prisoners.

These steps give some plausibility to the argument of people who never go near a prison that the inmates are somehow being rehabilitated. It is becoming painfully clear, however, that no such result ensues. Sixty per cent of the prison population in the United States is made up of repeaters, and we spend a vast sum of money to ensure the continuance of this figure. We spend it on cages, and caged human beings behave as they might be expected to behave, since there are not enough Bonnivards to rise spiritually above the gray stone walls and steel bars. Like a gambler who remains a gambler after paying his losses, a criminal remains a criminal after doing his time, and often his technique is improved after associating so intimately with his betters in the profession.

There must be something wrong, and it lies at the center of our conception of crime and its treatment. In 1790 Quakers had reason to feel that prison could be a place for meditation, silence, and work, and in comparison with prior sanctions the new system must have seemed merciful and not vengeful. But they have let 160 years go by without actively reviewing the central idea of punishment and without fully realizing that punishment, however inflicted, is still vengeance. Death, torture, and imprisonment in their turn have neither prevented crime nor cured criminals, and the reason is that they have all been inflicted in the form of punishment. It is about time to find a new idea, and it is being found. George Bernard Shaw, in his essay "The Crime of Imprisonment," shows that even the death penalty—which is only the most dramatic form of punishment—should be inflicted without vengeance. So long as we allow judicial killing, he says, the sane and passionate murderer should rarely if ever be executed, but the hardened and unregenerate killers should, like hopeless idiots, be sympathetically, apologetically, painlessly, and effectively removed from society and returned to the dust from which they sprung.

The Quaker peace testimony teaches us to absorb violence without returning it and by presenting an opponent with a peaceful example to lead him out of his violence. To educate, in its best sense. Such education arises if vengeance drops out. This is the idea that is beginning to make way in penology. American Quakers are no longer, as they were in 1790, in a position to enact a new penology into law, but for whatever power they have they should see the problem clearly. Penology does not need more palliatives such as correspondence courses, classes in knitting or weaving, or even dutiful visitation. It needs an overturn from the bottom and a new base to rest on.

In every separate penological system there should be an institution not called a prison, without walls or armed guards, where each inmate works an eight-hour day either at a useful task or in learning a trade, where no uniform but work clothes is required, where family visits are allowed each Sunday under attractive and not humiliating conditions, where unrestricted reading is allowed and encouraged, and where every sociological aid, including psychiatry, is available for the training and social reconstruction of the inmates. There is such an institution for men at Chino, California, one for women at Muncy, Pennsylvania, and a few others. To those who feel that if prisons are made attractive, large numbers of people will try to get into them, it is a full answer that the inmates do not have their liberty. They will feel that they are being punished merely because they are in detention, until they realize that an effort is being made to do for them something that they have hitherto been unable to do for themselves.

It is safe to say that almost half the present prison population could be so trusted and would benefit from such a program. The others would need greater restraint, and some will have to be kept permanently in maximum security fortresses, at least until we are wiser and surer in our treatment. Results are showing already and the idea need only grow. Society is now able to give a clean receipt for a few prisoners' payment of their debt, and these few leave without stigma and without further menace to a society that has done well for them and for itself.

Such a system cannot be said to be sentimental, but the present one is, since revenge is one of the strongest and most expensive sentiments in man. And in no true moral sense is it less a crime than the crime it punishes. Imprisonment will remain punishment until it stops passively watching a man do his time and actively works to remake him into a useful human being. It is much to show a man that the most bitter and relentless punishment occurs within himself, and to know that in the long run the punisher of others punishes himself the most. It is dangerous to think in terms of right and wrong when dealing with other people: the question should be one of the distance we can see.

Prisons and Prisoners
BY
HENRY VAN ETTEN

IX

Prisons and Prisoners

BY

HENRY VAN ETTEN

Agent-General for French organization engaged in the field of juvenile delinquency. Active in prison work in France for over thirty years.

BECAUSE OF THE numerous prison sentences they had to suffer, it is certain that the attention of the first Quakers was drawn to penal problems as the movement launched by George Fox spread throughout England. Thousands of Quakers were soon arrested and thrown into horrible prisons. George Fox was the first, and he was put in prison for the first time when he was twenty-five years old. Prisons must have been about the only resting place in his life, because he spent more than six years in them at different times, and it was only due to his exceptionally robust nature that he was able to resist the cruel treatment he underwent. His staying in prison did not stop his apostolic fervor. From there he wrote to pastors, magistrates, to his opponents, and to his friends. The filth of the cells was frightful. At Launceston, the floor was covered with a mess of mud and urine, in which one sank to the ankles. At Scarborough Castle he was imprisoned for nearly three years. During his imprisonment at Worcester he wrote several books and pamphlets.

In 1650 while he was in prison in Derby—he was twenty-six years old—he wrote to the judges on the subject "concerning their putting men to death for [stealing] cattle and money and small matters." "I laid before the judges," he said, "what a hurtful thing it was that the prisoners would lie so long in jail, showing how that they learned badness one of another in talking of their bad deeds, and therefore speedy justice should be done." George Fox, in these lines, and without knowing it, was proposing a whole program of penal reform, such as the selection of prisoners and the utility of speedy justice; a program which, after three hundred years, has not yet been applied even by the most civilized nations.

We have to recall that it was in the Tower of London that the best known of Fox's disciples, William Penn, wrote his well-known book *No Cross, No Crown*. He was twenty-four years old. During this captivity he sent the following message to the King: "Tell the King that the Tower is the worst argument in the world to convince me, for whoever is in the wrong, those who use force for religion never could be in the right." King Charles II, tired of the affair, released him on July 28th, 1669. Penn was victorious!

Later on, when William Penn had founded his colony of Pennsylvania (1681 to 1683), he submitted a document to the first Assembly gathered on December 4th, 1682. He approved of imprisonment as a method of coercion, but he disapproved of the idleness in which the prisoners were kept. "All prisons shall be workhouses for felons, vagrants, and loose and idle persons: whereof one shall be in every county. . . . All prisoners shall be bailable by sufficient sureties, unless for capital offences, where the proof is evident, or the presumption great. . . . All prisons shall be free, as to fees, food and lodgings."

The laws of William Penn substituted imprisonment and fines for the death penalty for those who were guilty of a crime. It is true that at that time, two hundred crimes were punishable by death. In his colonies, Penn limited the number of crimes punishable by death to two, murder and treason. And it can be said that, thanks to him, the American penal system has been softened during the last three centuries.

It was around the year 1776 that American Friends started to be interested in prisons and prisoners. An association called

"The Philadelphia Society for Relieving Distressed Prisoners" was created in Philadelphia, but because of the war it could not function until 1787. The association was in charge of the administration of Walnut Street Prison in 1790. The United States Constitution forbade "cruel and unusual punishments." And with the abolition of "bloody punishments" (beating, mutilations, pilloring, branding, hanging, drowning, and quartering), the prison became more and more the place of prolonged residence for which it had not been intended. The horrible conditions of the jails, physically and morally, started to move the charitable souls at the end of the eighteenth century!

The Walnut Street Prison was originally intended as a place of reform and had been called the "penitentiary." Each cell opened onto a small garden for the prisoners' walks, and each of the prisoners had to do a certain amount of work. The purpose of this solitary confinement was to give the prisoner the opportunity to reflect, meditate, and repent. These principles were far in advance of the ideas of that time.

Solitary confinement drew the attention of the authorities in other countries. The following passages are from a book published in France about forty years later, in which the situation is well summarized:

> The first thought of reform in American prisons came from a religious sect in Pennsylvania. The Quakers, whose principles were against all shedding of blood, had always protested against the barbarous laws which the colonies had inherited from the mother country. In 1786 their voice began to be heard and beginning from this period, the death penalty, mutilation, and the whip were successively abolished in nearly all cases by the courts of Pennsylvania. From then on the plight of the convicts was alleviated. Imprisonment was substituted for corporal punishment, and tribunals were authorized by law to impose solitary confinement day and night on all those guilty of capital offences. It was then that the Walnut Street Prison was set up. The convicts were sorted out and grouped according to their crimes, and individual cells were built for those condemned by the courts of justice to absolute isolation. Individual cells were also used as a means of breaking up the resistance of those who refused to submit to the discipline of the prison. The solitary convicts did not

work. The innovation was good but incomplete, and the impossibility of grouping the convicts under appropriate classifications has since then become apparent, and solitary confinement with no work whatsoever to do has been ruled out by experience. . . . The Walnut Street Prison regime failed to bring about any of the good effects that were hoped for. It had two main defects, i.e., convicts who worked together were further corrupted by contact with each other just as those who were completely isolated were further corrupted by idleness. The real merit of its founders lies in having been instrumental in the abolishment of the bloody laws of Pennsylvania and in arousing public attention to set up a new system of imprisonment.[1]

The deadly effects of severe solitary confinement without labor did not prevent Pennsylvania from continuing the attempt in other places than Philadelphia. In 1827 the Penitentiary of Pittsburgh started to receive prisoners, but without success, especially since it was known that in the new prison of Auburn in the State of New York, the prisoners were working together during the daytime and were separated at night. The question of solitary confinement without labor was then submitted to a new examination. A commission of investigation brought pressure on public opinion in spite of some opposition.

Rival of New York, Pennsylvania was jealous to keep the position which her advanced civilization gave her among the other states of the American Union. According to de Beaumont and de Tocqueville, "she adopted a system that fitted at the same time the austerity of her moral and her philanthropic feelings, she cast off solitary confinement without labor, as experience from elsewhere has demonstrated its bad effects, and she kept the absolute separation of the prisoners, a punishment which does not need the help of corporal punishment to be effective."

The new penitentiary of Cherry Hill in Philadelphia became a combination of Pittsburgh and Auburn. The Pittsburgh idea of solitary day and night confinement was kept, and into the solitary cell was introduced the idea of labor from Auburn. This revolution in the prison organization of Pennsylvania was

[1] de Beaumont and de Tocqueville, *On the Penitentiary System of the United States* (Philadelphia: translation by Francis Lieber, 1833).

immediately followed by a general reform of criminal laws. All the penalties were softened. The death penalty was abolished in all circumstances, except in the case of murder with premeditation. One can realize by the above how much the religious influence, and particularly the Quaker one, was felt in these new conceptions at that time. To separate the prisoners as a common good sense demanded and to classify them by categories to avoid contamination had led to a rigorous system of confinement. It was considered that this separation, which prevented the bad ones from harming the others, was favorable to the prisoner. Confined in solitude, he was then able to think. Facing his crime he starts hating it, and in this confinement he should be assailed by remorse. One can well see how this conclusion of well-intentioned people came about, but naturally they did not know anything at this time about human psychology and man's instinctive reactions. Today there are still some defenders of the solitary confinement system (with labor, of course). Solitary confinement without labor, although this has been abandoned little by little, leads to madness or to relapse into crime after leaving prison. Work fills the solitary cell with interest: "It tires the body and calms the soul," according to the authors already mentioned. They also wrote:

> Pennsylvania is perhaps the only state of the Union which is still protesting against the use of corporal punishment, and this has been banished from their prisons. Quakers do not cease to protest against the inhumanity of this penalty. Joined in their philanthropic concerns, the eloquent voice of Edward Livingstone, can be heard. He also banished this kind of discipline from his penitentiary code ... but their words found little echo from most of the states of the Union, and today all the new penitentiaries, with the exception of the one in Philadelphia, seek in this kind of punishment a means of keeping order and discipline.[2]

To end these paragraphs on the Quaker influence in American prisons, de Beaumont and de Tocqueville, making a comparison with French prisons at that time, state that "the prison in which the system is corrupting, is at the same time dreadful

[2] *Ibid.*

for the life of the prisoners. In our country, the prisoners confined in our main prisons are dying in the proportion of one out of fourteen. In the penitentiaries in America an average of one out of 49 die." The authors ask themselves in conclusion, if the exceptional harshness of the American penitentiaries (perpetual isolation, absolute silence, uniformity of inflexible regulations, etc.) are not "in fact: regulations full of humanity?" It must be remembered that these lines were written about 1830, during a period when French prisons were horrible cesspools, to use the terms of de Beaumont and de Tocqueville. The so-called "Pennsylvania System," which, under more or less Quaker influence, made a real progress at that time, gave way to some more modern systems, progressively in accordance with the discoveries of science.

Let us go back a little and consider again the problem of prisons through Quaker experience. We must remember that the work undertaken by the Friends was essentially the result of individual actions and not at all the result of official decisions coming from the Society of Friends. Dr. Auguste Jorns says in his book, *The Quakers as Pioneers in Social Work*: "The Society had early emphasized the close connection between poverty, neglect of education, alcoholism, and crime, and had recognized the actual encouragement of crime resulting from the deficiencies in the laws and their execution." For instance, the Quaker John Bellers, born in 1654 and considered the pioneer of modern Christian socialism, wrote: "It is affecting to consider that the Bodies of many Poor, which might and should be Temples for the Holy Ghost to dwell in, are the Receptacles so much of Vice and Vermine." At the same period George Fox was writing in his *Journal:* "Those who are rich should procure work for the poor so as to preserve them from temptation." [3]

In 1661 in England there were nearly 8000 Quakers in prison. Margaret Fox, wife of George Fox, one day wrote to the King: "If they continue to put in prison so many poor fathers and

[3] Dr. Auguste Jorns, *Quakers as Pioneers in Social Work* (New York: Macmillan, 1931).

merchants, now that the season is coming, who is going to hold the ploughs and who is going to sow the corn for these families?" They were treated like civil law criminals, and while the other prisoners gave money to the jailer in order to ease their pains, the Friends refused to do so for reasons of conscience.

Although George Fox accepted the death penalty as a right punishment for murder, John Bellers was demanding its abolishment. It is probably the first time in history that the suppression of the death penalty has been claimed publicly, even before the Italian Beccaria had asked for it in his book *Dei delitti e delle pene* (of murders and punishments), published in 1764 and considered to be the first appeal made on this subject. Like Fox, he considered that the prisoners should work according to their capacity, through an apprenticeship, and thus be prepared to enter industry when they come out of prison. Until the appearance of John Howard (born in 1726) and except for a few voices emanating from groups or individuals, it can be said that nothing concrete was done in England.

John Howard was not a Quaker; he came from a well-to-do family and was made Great Sheriff of Bedford, which enabled him to inspect the local prisons and to see their conditions. In 1774, he presented himself at the House of Commons and asked for reforms. A law was then voted but had no effect. In 1777 he published his principal book on the penal reform. (*The State of the Prisons in England and Wales, with Preliminary Observation and an Account of some Foreign Prisons.*) Nevertheless his efforts remained very limited in spite of his passionate faith in the cause. "He considered himself like the digger who prepares the materials for the men of genius who are going to employ them." It depended on the Friends to put in practice the principles of John Howard. He worked in close contact with members of the Society of Friends, the most important of whom was Dr. John Fothergill, who visited American prisons in 1744–45, assisted by some "Quaker Ministers" and by Catherine Phillips. There was also Thomas Shillitoe, who was especially interested in the spiritual and physical needs of the prisoners; but as it was a strict personal work it could not bear many fruits. The problem was so wide that individual help could do no more than bring relief to a few persons. It was necessary to wait more than twenty-five years after the death of John Howard to see the beginning of the organization which was at last going to bring forward the most indispensable reforms.

We are here at the period of that remarkable woman, Elizabeth Fry. She was born in 1780 and was the great-great-granddaughter of the Quaker theologian Robert Barclay, and daughter of John Gurney, banker in Norwich. At the age of seventeen she started visiting sick people and she organized and directed a small school for the children of the neighborhood until her marriage to Joseph Fry on August 19, 1800. She was a good housekeeper and the mother of eleven children. Her tireless Christian interest in helping others never slackened. Her first field of action happened to be the women's section at the London prison of Newgate. Six big rooms around the courtyard were the quarters reserved to the women. Supervision and service were assumed by men only. The prisoners lived all together without distinction according to age or crime. If they had money they could buy supplementary food and alcohol. Order and cleanness were unknown at Newgate and the only occupations of the prisoners were gambling, drinking, quarreling, and fighting.

It was through a French Quaker living in America, Stephen Grellet, that Elizabeth Fry took an interest in Newgate prison. Grellet came to Europe during the winter of 1812–1813, when he visited the famous prison and saw how horrible it was. He went everywhere, from the filthy infirmary to the dirtiest cells and from these to the rooms of those sentenced to death. He was struck by the children who were imprisoned with their mothers. They were badly fed, covered with rags; they were left to themselves, without care or attention. Grellet went to his friend Elizabeth Fry and told her about his visit, asking her help for the unfortunate children. The next day she brought to the prison a big bale of clothing for the children. The work of her life had started.

Newgate was built for 500 prisoners; in 1813 it contained 822. There were 300 women with a great number of children and only two warders to care for them. At the beginning Elizabeth Fry and some friends could only bring a little help to some very special "cases." It was only in 1816 that she was able to start doing an organized piece of work. The first step was the creation of a small school for the children of the prisoners and for the 44 young delinquents there among the boys' group. A worthy and well-educated woman was chosen by the prisoners themselves, from among the women, as teacher for the school. The next step was the foundation, in 1817, at Newgate of the "Association for the Improvement of Women Prisoners." First it was composed of a pastor and his wife and eleven members of the Society of Friends. In spite of the skepticism of the authorities, a general meeting of all women prisoners was held, during which the association's aims were explained. Elizabeth Fry pointed out that the association had no power whatever, and that its only desire was to help the prisoners. The prisoners had to establish their own rules and choose their own delegates. The proposition was accepted right away, and groups were formed immediately, each of them under the supervision of a woman prisoner. A matron, who henceforth lived at the prison, was hired by the association. When all this was arranged, a workroom was organized and all kinds of clothes were made. At the first call, seventy women came in to work, and a month had barely passed before all kinds of visitors came to Newgate, against the desire and will of Elizabeth Fry.

The "Corporation of London" came to visit the prison and what they found was beyond their imagination. Instead of the "hell on earth" they had expected to see, they entered into peaceful rooms where the prisoners were busy with needlework and cutting. The experience was sanctioned by the authorities and the association had the right to punish if it was necessary. Subsidies were granted to cover the expense of the association. The money earned by the prisoners was put aside for their release from prison. But small amounts of money were given them by Elizabeth Fry, that they might buy some extras at the canteen. To avoid accusations of entering into competition with local trade, Elizabeth Fry wisely sent nearly all the work to Australia, where there was a life convicts' colony.

Lectures on the Bible were given to the prisoners by Elizabeth Fry amidst great silence. It was said that an expression of gravity and self-respect could be seen on their faces, as if these women were conscious of an improvement in their own temper, behavior, and position. In 1818 our Friend was called before a committee at the House of Commons, as John Howard had been called many years before. She had to fight her natural shyness to answer the summons. Whereas John Howard had defended the harshness of solitary confinement, Elizabeth Fry fought it with all her strength. For her it was a fatal mistake and an inhuman measure. At the time of this interview she had only two requests to formulate: to replace the men wardens by women and to have the prisons for women completely separated from the men's quarters. She insisted on the necessity of teaching and practicing handiwork so that when the women were freed they would be able to earn their living honestly. She seized the opportunity to speak in favor of a selection among the prisoners according to the seriousness of the crimes in order to separate the murderers and prostitutes from those who were in prison for debts. Her idea was to keep the women together during the day for work and meals or leisure and to separate them at night.

It can be seen that Elizabeth Fry came to the same conclusion as the creators of the American prison at Auburn: life in common during the day and separation at night. Though she never made any special studies of penitentiary systems, her heart and her intelligence were against confinement in cells, and she came to a conclusion which in civilized countries has never since been greatly altered.

The reforms she asked were received with a certain skepticism and the Commission's report was rather negative. Mrs. Ansermoz-Dubois says in her book on Elizabeth Fry, published in Switzerland in 1950: "The English government had two measures which were radical and not expensive: transportation and hanging." The efforts of the association were no longer limited to Newgate. However, it was only in 1836 that the founder was able to write in her journal: "I believe that every jail is now being visited." Mrs. Fry to her great confusion was then very well known. "It is marvelous in my eyes that a poor instrument should have been the apparent cause of setting forward such a work."

A prison penalty was often followed by transportation to places where conditions were such that the little improvement that was gained in the prison was then lost completely. Upon their arrival at their destination, the convicts were directed to farms or tracts of undeveloped land where they were required as "workmen." No more were they under government protection. The departures for New South Wales produced some shocking scenes, particularly among the women. Fights and shrieks of revolt always preceded the embarkment, and the convicts had to be chained before going on board.

Elizabeth Fry soon protested against such methods and offered to take in hand the entire convoy organization of the sailing ships. She insisted upon two conditions: the suppression of irons and all other means of force, and the transfer of the women in closed carriages in order to avoid the insults of the crowd. Matrons were engaged to accompany the convicts to Australia and a complete organization was set up inside the ships. They repartitioned the groups by cabin, and material was distributed so that the prisoners could continue their work. There was also a school for children under seven years accompanying their mothers. Success came with the first departure; it was with silence and dignity that the first convoy left England. From that day on (in 1818) and until her death in 1845, Elizabeth Fry, with very few exceptions, supervised all the prison convoys of women who were to be transported. There were one hundred and six of these, and more than twelve thousand women were deported in them. Before leaving, each deportee received a gift —a bag marked with her number, containing a Bible and some other useful articles. A small library was installed on board and books were lent to prisoners as a reward for good behavior.

As a convinced Christian, Elizabeth Fry could not admit the legitimacy of the death penalty. She believed with all her heart in "the seed of God in every man," however outcast or fallen he might be. She refused to admit that men could take away a life that was given by God. With the Friends she claimed the abolition of the death penalty. The Epistles of London Yearly Meeting of 1818, and later of 1830 and 1847, show that the Society of Friends in England took a firm position in the face of this problem.

From the beginning of her real ministry, Elizabeth Fry was called upon to visit the women sentenced to death. Several times she took desperate steps to try to save a life. This only strengthened her will, and she continued to fight for the complete suppression of the death penalty. The first of all associations for the abolition of capital punishment was founded in 1808, mainly by Quakers. They first tried to obtain an attenuation in the laws. In 1830, a great popular movement was launched to abolish the death penalty for forgers, and the Friends gathered a thousand signatures from bankers in all parts of England for a petition to Parliament, insisting on the point that fear of death had never prevented crime. This, they stated, could be seen from the statistics in other countries where capital punishment had been abolished and crimes were decreasing. The 1830 agitation brought, two years later, an Act of Parliament suppressing the death penalty for forgery, and in 1837, when Queen Victoria acceded to the throne, the number of crimes punishable by death had decreased from one hundred and fifty, at the beginning of the century, to ten.

Criminality among youth had likewise drawn the attention of Friends. A "Society for Lessening the Causes of Juvenile Delinquency in the Metropolis" was helped by Quakers like Peter Bradford and William Allen, the well-known philanthropist and scientist. Their investigations brought to light the fact that in London thousands of children were living exclusively by means of robbery. Hunger, slums, lack of work, and a minimum of education were the causes of crime and delinquency.

Elizabeth Fry had enlisted to her cause several members of her family—her brother-in-law T. F. Buxton, and his wife, her two brothers—Joseph John Gurney and Samuel Gurney—and her friends Stephen Grellet, W. Allen, P. Belford, and others. Their writings and her own gave a very clear picture of the penal reforms for which Quakers were asking at that time.

Dr. Auguste Jorns in his book summarized the two principal points supported by the Friends as follows: "The demands of the Quakers are based upon two presumptions: 1) Even the convicted criminal has *certain rights*. 2) The purpose which is of greatest importance to society is the reform of the convict." [4] To avoid the dangers of promiscuity, Friends asked for the selection and separation of prisoners but without going, except for some special cases, to the harshness of solitary confinement, "for man was created a social being." To forbid the prisoners to speak, as well as to darken their cells and to chain them up, were measures without good effect. Here it will be seen once more how greatly English Quakers differed from Americans, who had proposed and maintained the benefit of the strict cellular system. Experience has demonstrated the harms of solitary confinement and it has been in some measures given up now by most of the civilized countries.

According to the Quakers—in this they were the precursors—the concept of punishment had to give way to concepts of reformation and education, and as a corollary, the necessity of bettering the penal institutions. Elementary instruction was to be given to the prisoners, as in handicraft work. At that time 87 per cent of the prisoners were illiterate, and it is quite natural that Friends insisted on introducing the so-called Lancaster System into the prisons. Teaching the prisoners to read was not only a means of elevating their intelligence but it also gave them the possibility of reading and studying the Bible, which Friends believed was indispensable to a moral and useful life. The nomination of chaplains to visit the men and women prisoners was asked for as well as a better recruitment of supervisory personnel.

Elizabeth Fry was sixty-five years old when she died. Fortunately her death did not stop the movement in favor of penal reforms. In 1866 an association was founded in London which is still very powerful and known all over the world: "The Howard League for Penal Reform." On its committee as well as in its other branches there are a great number of Quakers and a well-appreciated magazine is published.

[4] *Ibid.*

After the first world war, two members of the Society of Friends, Stephen Hobhouse and Fenner Brockway, who had suffered imprisonment as conscientious objectors, were moved by their experience to make a detailed survey of the whole prison system in England as it then existed in 1922. They published their findings in an important work: *English Prisons Today*. The closing words of Hobhouse and Brockway's book have lost no truth despite the passing of more than a quarter of a century:

> In our prisons we put away men for our own convenience, and for the sake of financial economy, control them by mechanical methods, which . . . deteriorate their own characters and dissipate their inheritance in humanity . . .[5]

We cannot leave England and pass to other countries without mentioning a few well-known names. The first one is the name of Geraldine Cadbury, wife of Barry Cadbury. She was a magistrate and devoted her life to juvenile delinquents and youth in moral danger. She died in 1941, leaving behind her an unforgettable memory. The second name is that of Margery Fry, no longer a member of the Society of Friends but in lineal descent from Quakers. She is actually a world-wide authority on penal problems. And finally, there is R. Duncan Fairn, Assistant Commissioner and Inspector of Prisons and recently appointed Director of the English Penitentiary Administration. These three examples show to what extent the British Friends continue to be interested in prison problems. They are representative of a great number of Quakers who are prison visitors, lecturers, and voluntary school teachers in the penitentiaries or in institutions for young delinquents. In addition there are at present forty-eight Friends who are prison chaplains. A large number are magistrates and quite a few are probation officers. Following is a statement describing the present work of the Penal Reform Committee of the Society of Friends in England:

[5]. Stephen M. Hobhouse and A. Fenner Brockway, *English Prisons To-day*. (London: Labour Research Dept., 1922).

The Committee aims at a constructive approach to the problems of penal reform and seeks to promote measures for the prevention of crime and for the wiser treatment of offenders. Its work is rooted in the conviction that the wrong-doer must be understood and not merely condemned and punished. To understand the wrong-doer means to understand the complex causes of crime and delinquency, the character and heredity of the individual, and his social and economic surroundings. Treatment should help to reform the wrong-doer and so to transform him into a useful and responsible citizen. . . .

In France, the author of this paper was first helped by a French Friend, Phebe Borghesio, and then by a Dutch Friend, Gerda Kappenburg, and a prison service was started through the "Centre Quaker International" of Paris in 1924. Soon afterwards a fourth person, Marie Kaftal, joined them. For nearly three years this service took special care of the women's prison of St. Lazare in Paris. Gerda Kappenburg's efforts were soon directed toward a program of general reform of the French prisons. In 1926, she and the author founded a neutral committee called "Committee for the Diminution of Crime," and the latter became General Secretary under the presidency of the highest French authority on criminal matters, Professor Henri Donnedieu de Vabres, who died in February, 1952. By public lectures and articles in the papers, by the creation in 1935 of the first specialized magazine ever published on delinquent youth, by improvements inside the prison, by visiting the young prisoners in the penitentiaries, the work has been carried on.

At present, the French Quaker Group has women visitors who visit the prisons in Paris and in Le Havre; and a man visitor in Lyons who is secretary to the Help Committee for Discharged Prisoners.

During the war and the occupation, the Quaker Center in Paris organized a relief service for the persons who were arrested first by the French authorities, then by the Germans. Although this work differed slightly from that which had preceded it, nevertheless thousands of men and women were saved from starvation and disease, thanks to the "Quaker parcels" distributed in six or seven prisons and concentration camps of the Department of the Seine, and in the towns of Bordeaux, Nancy and Dijon. From 1941 to 1944, over 54,000 parcels were distributed in the Paris area alone. After the retreat of the German armies, aid to the French prisoners was increased with the help of English and American Quakers. This continued until 1946. It must be added that during the occupation, from 1943 onwards, a relief service for the prisoners of "common law" was created in four Parisian prisons and in the four Centers for young delinquents in Paris.

American Quakers had also organized a similar service in the southern occupation zone at Marseilles, Montauban, Toulouse, and Perpignan until the entry of the United States into the war. Continued by non-Quaker Committee this service afterwards became a part of "Secours Quaker" in Paris in 1944–1945. Before closing these notes on this special prison activity in France (mainly but not only relief), it is good to note that the Quaker conviction that there is "something of God in every man" was also evidenced in this aid which, from one day to the next, in August, 1944, passed from the victims of the German police to the victims of the French police and mob—the French people who were suspected of being German sympathizers. Thanks to the sympathetic understanding of the new French authorities, there was not one day in this difficult change-over period when the relief efforts in the prisons were stopped.

The Quaker approach to prisons and prisoners has also been affected during and after the last two wars by the large number of "conscientious objectors" sent to prison. The treatment meted out to objectors sentenced to prison in England in World War I was particularly hard. They stayed sometimes for years in cells just large enough for a board which served as a bed. Absolute silence was enforced. Lloyd George declared that these men should be placed in a position of as much hardship and discomfort as possible. Those convicted were made to serve several successive sentences, the first being generally for two years. A new refusal of military service led to a second sentence, then to a third. Often, in the end, the prisoners' spirits were broken despite their moral resistance. Would organizations representing the imprisoned defaulters have to put all their efforts in the liberation of the prisoners and the amelioration of their conditions?

The Society of Friends hesitated. Some refused to make direct efforts for the liberation of the defaulters; others, on the contrary, wanted to act forcefully in the name of civil and religious liberty to obtain their unconditional freedom. Finally it seemed to the Quakers that they should leave to others the task of protesting in favor of the prisoners. The liberation of Quakers only was not the aim to be achieved and, moreover, the Society of Friends demanded the total suppression of the regulations and not simply a "right" organization. However, in 1918, London Yearly Meeting addressed a call to the conscience of the nation for the immediate liberation of the objectors. The number of deaths increased every month. In January, 1919, there were still 1,500 men in prison, and it was only July 30th, eight months after the end of the war, that all the objectors were released. The treatment given to the conscientious objectors has been considerably improved since World War I thanks to the courage and self-abnegation of the 1916–1918 objectors.

In the United States, in 1917, there were 4,000 unwilling to serve in the armed forces for reasons of conscience. They underwent more or less prolonged captivity in military prisons, and were released during the years 1919 and 1920. The law contained an exemption clause for the objectors who were known to belong to religious or pacifist groups such as Quakers and Mennonites, but this clause was seldom rightly applied. During World War II, special camps were created for the objectors. In July, 1943, there were a little more than 6,000 men; 700 were working in hospitals, on farms or on agriculture projects. At the same time, 700 objectors were detained in prison for periods of from nine months to five years for several causes. In May, 1944, 3,000 men were in prison out of an approximate total of 10,000 officially enlisted. Of this number, 594 were Friends.

As part of the American Friends Service Committee of Philadelphia, a group called the "Prison Service Committee" served the cause of the objectors in prison. It created a new interest among Friends in prisons and prison problems. In fact a great number of American Friends are today interested and actively engaged in penal work.

From this survey it can be seen that the efforts undertaken for the amelioration of the conditions of prisoners and the reform of penal systems during the last three centuries were for the most part due to Quaker initiative of private origin, and they have influenced favorably several governments in Europe as well as in the United States. Practical application of their religious faith, personal conviction expressed in daily events, total respect for the human life, acknowledgement of the "light" which is in every man, these were the reasons for the actions undertaken. And they were undertaken without consideration of financial possibilities, or of the great difficulties presented by the public authorities, or of the opposition of public opinion.

Starting as volunteers "under concern," but without special training, Quakers little by little have had to follow the progress in modern technique and have had to look for personnel among "concerned" men and women, who were specially trained for these human and social tasks. The essential point is to keep this "Quaker spirit," which is so necessary to the success of efforts undertaken on even a small scale. The Quaker initiative has served and should always serve as an example for those in official positions.

The work in the prisons remains one of the great "testimonies" of the Society of Friends in the world. May it remain faithful to the special call launched during the centuries in obedience to the work of Christ: *"I was in prison and ye came unto me."* (Matthew XXV, 36.)

Science

BY
KATHLEEN LONSDALE

X

Science

BY

KATHLEEN LONSDALE

Professor of Chemistry and Head of the Department of Crystallography at London University, Fellow of the Royal Society of London, author of many papers in the field of science.

AN ENGLISH QUAKER records that, a few months ago, he was sitting in a restaurant eating his lunch when a young and agreeable couple came and sat at his table. The girl opened a daily picture-paper and, pointing to a headline, said to her boy friend, "Look! 'Seven Quakers go to Moscow.'" "What are Quakers?" asked the boy. "They're religious," replied the girl; "queer people who wait until the spirit moves them." The boy murmured and turned his attention to more glamourous features of the paper.

It may be that some Quakers themselves would be puzzled to explain why it is that a small religious sect of supposedly "queer" views and practices has attracted to itself such a high percentage of scientists, as undoubtedly it has. Judging by statistics covering the last 150 years, a Quaker, or a man of Quaker birth, has some twenty or thirty times the chance of election to the Fellowship of the Royal Society (the highest scientific honor bestowable in Great Britain) as his fellow countrymen in general. This is not, let us hasten to add, one of the reasons why scientists become Quakers! Nor is it simply a question of Quakerism being, or having become, "respectable," so that Quakers are drawn mainly from the professional or upper middle class. It applied even when they were not so respectable.

From the very first, there has been a close parallel between the attitude of Quakers toward authority and experience in religion and the attitude of modern science. Modern science may indeed be said to have been struggling for expression in the early seventeenth century, struggling against the centuries-old habits of the Aristotelian school of thought and against the dead weight of authoritative theological dogma, an authority backed by the temporal and political power of the Church. Galileo, born in 1564, and Kepler, nearly eight years his junior, used the new scientific instrument, the telescope, to make astronomical observations which convinced them of the truth of the Copernican theory that the earth moves round the sun. Of Kepler it is said that he founded a new astronomy in which physical laws replaced arbitrary hypotheses. Galileo, no less eminent, is perhaps known as much for his conflict with the Inquisition as for his experimental researches. But the point is that he was the champion of the experimental and of the deduction of physical laws from experiment, as against the conception of science as a rounded body of complete knowledge.

The medieval schoolmen had taken Aristotle's scheme of the universe, concentric spheres with the earth at the center, and had built upon it a system of theology whose truth they believed to be bound up in the truth of the cosmic theory on which it was based. Aristotle was not nearly so dogmatic as those who followed him, and he himself believed in the continual unfolding of truth by means of investigation, but how could theologians permit experimental observations to cast doubt on the correctness of theology? Galileo was therefore silenced, but no power on earth could prevent the slow realization that his observations had been correct and his deductions sound, and that the *only* sound theory was one that could stand the test of experiment.

Kepler was a German; Galileo an Italian; but it was a Frenchman of science, Descartes, a devout Catholic, a contemporary of Galileo but completely out of sympathy with him, who nevertheless carried on the torch. In his *Rules for the Direction of the Mind* (1628) he demanded that the investigation of any problem should not be dominated by the thought or argument of others, but by what we ourselves see clearly or deduce with certainty. A mathematician is not someone who has learned by heart the proofs elaborated by other scholars, but is one who has the intellectual talent to resolve mathematical problems himself. Descartes put more faith in intuition and in deduction from intuition than in experience, although he realized that experience also added to knowledge; but he insisted that a sound scientific investigation could be based only on correct first principles, and these first principles, or axioms, are given by intuition alone. This intuition he defines as "the undoubting conception of an unclouded and attentive mind, which springs from the light of reason. . . . Thus each individual can have intuition of the fact that he exists, and that he thinks." Moreover, everything that claims to be the starting-point of knowledge must be questioned, since traditional beliefs, commonly accepted ideas, the very facts of direct observation, may be illusory. The one thing that is beyond doubt is doubt itself, and doubt is an act of thinking, which presupposes a thinker. *Cogito, ergo sum.* "I think, therefore I am."

He goes on to argue from this the existence of God, but this did not save him from attack, this time by Protestant theologians, who hinted that his new philosophy was essentially atheistic. Descartes' philosophy and the consequent contributions to science that he made, though incomplete and incorrect in many ways, were typical of a new attitude of mind, a new methodology of science; and it was this new spirit of inquiry that led the way, in the second half of the seventeenth century, to those discussions among men of science which resulted in the formation of the Royal Society. The Fellows of the Society were directed to apply their studies "to the further promoting by the authority of experiments the sciences of natural things and of useful arts, to the glory of God the Creator and the advantage of the human race."

The early Quakers did not necessarily know of all these new currents of thought, although some of them did, for two of them were among the Founder Fellows of the Royal Society, but they were part of the current themselves. Their approach to religion resembled the new approach to science. They believed, as Quakers still believe, that religion should not be a matter of the acceptance of dogma, or of a closed theological system however sacred, but a personal experience, a way of life. George Fox, who claimed that his knowledge of the ways of God was experimental, and who may be said to be the founder of Quakerism, was described by his contemporary, William Penn, as "a man that God endued with a clear and wonderful depth, a discerner of others' spirits, and very much a master of his own. . . . I have been surprised at his questions and answers in natural things; that whilst he was ignorant of useless and sophistical science, he had in him the foundation of useful and commendable knowledge, and cherished it everywhere."

Quakers would also join with Descartes in the necessity for clear thinking on the subject of first principles, on the importance of questioning commonly accepted or traditional ideas, of avoiding credulity and superstition, even though they might not be able to follow him in all of his deductions. Above all they do not regard knowledge, whether of truth or any other aspect of God, as closed, but as continually capable of expansion. One of the "Queries" that is expected to be read in Quaker Meetings for Worship at least once a year asks: "Are you striving to develop your mental powers and to use them to the Glory of God? Are you loyal to the truth and do you keep your mind open to new light, from whatever quarter it may arise?"

These questions are singularly reminiscent of the direction to the Fellows of the Royal Society quoted here, and of the question that Benjamin Franklin put to would-be members of his Junta, the predecessor of the American Philosophical Society of Philadelphia, as to whether they were willing to seek the truth, and having found it, to accept it for themselves and to communicate it to others?

It is not without significance that the early Quakers who went about the country preaching became known as "Publishers of

Truth" or "Children of Light," and that many of them had previously belonged to a sect known as "Seekers."

It follows that from the very beginning there was no antagonism between Quakerism and the new scientific outlook. Quakers believed, as Rufus Jones has put it, that the "relation between God and man is direct, energizing, vital, and transforming, and as much a matter of experience and verification as sunlight." They invited others to share that experience. They had no dogma to defend, no authority to maintain, no superstitions to be attacked; and were able to accept, quite simply, those observations of scientists that were being made with the instruments of the times, insofar as they were confirmed or confirmable by independent investigation. Indeed, individual Quakers assisted greatly in the making of these experiments by their skill as instrument-makers, especially during the period when, like other nonconformits, they were excluded from the universities and learned professions. Men such as Thomas Tompion (1638–1713), Daniel Quare (1649–1724), and George Graham (1673–1751) had no doubt that in their construction of clocks and other apparatus they were working to the glory of God and the advancement of truth.

It may not be out of place here to mention that Friends were closely associated with the founding and organizing of the first British railways, and that it was a Friend, George Bradshaw (1801–1853), who issued the first collective railway timetable for the convenience of the public, thus encouraging the expectation that trains, one of the more beneficial products of a scientific age, would run on time! Early Friends carried their enthusiasm for experimentation even into their instrument-making, for it was another clockmaker, Benjamin Huntsman (1704–1776) who, needing better steel for watch springs, experimented on the making of steels and achieved a result upon which it has been difficult to improve, even up to modern times. Many Friends, indeed, have assisted in countless ways in the development of those mechanical contrivances which have so completely transformed modern civilizations, which have eased the lives of working men and women, and annihilated space; and which are now in danger of being so misused that human survival itself is imperiled.

The history of science dates back to the time when man began intelligently to study his environment for his own instruction and to use it for his own advantage. The road has been marked by milestones and there has been division of the ways. There have even been times when man has apparently lost his way. Lone workers then blazoned tracks through the jungle and set up signposts that others might follow. Superstition has stalked hand-in-hand with knowledge and technology: fire, sacrifice, and the smelting of ore for the making of tools; astronomy, astrology, and the charting of journeys by the use of the stars; herbs, witches, and the development of medicine. Knowledge itself has been put to evil as well as to good use. Herbs may be used to poison as well as to heal. Tools can be used for harmful as well as for good purposes. The very phrase "to throw a monkey-wrench in the works" illustrates that.

Many Friends, throughout the history of the Society, have been medical men, or have been concerned to apply medical knowledge on a national scale. In 1714, John Bellers wrote "An Essay Towards the Improvement of Physick By which the Lives of Many Thousands of the Rich as well as of the Poor may be Saved Yearly," and in *Quaker Way,* A. Ruth Fry has recorded the contents of this essay as follows:

His detailed suggestions were practical, including a record of each patient with treatment and results; a post-mortem on each death; an experimental hospital . . . another hospital for incurables where, by the patient's leave, experiments might be tried, any cures to be rewarded by the Government . . . the public provision of doctors in every hundred of the country and every parish of a city, to be paid by the overseers of the poor, and a public laboratory for preparing medicines and searching for new ones, even sending investigators to learn from Indians and Negroes.[1]

Indeed, as Ruth Fry points out, since the Army, the Navy, and the Church were all impossible professions for Quakers, med-

1. Anna Ruth Fry. *Quaker Way.* (London: Cassell & Company, 1933).

icine, which offers scope both for a scientific bent and for humanitarian satisfaction, was clearly likely to attract a high proportion of educated Friends.

These early Friends would have rejoiced, as Friends rejoice today, that many of the major plagues of mankind have been almost or completely wiped out, that deadly diseases can be cured, that infant mortality has been reduced in many countries to a small fraction of its former proportions and the normal expectation of life considerably increased, that crops have been improved by scientific study of growth conditions by the elimination of weeds and pests, and that the establishment of public health measures in many countries has greatly improved the physique and resistance to disease of the peoples of these countries. Many young Friends in recent years, particularly conscientious objectors, have served voluntarily as human guinea pigs to contribute to the alleviation or prevention of human disease. John Bellers would have approved.

A serious aberration of medical and physiological knowledge has occurred recently in the study and development of bacteriological and biological warfare. During the last war many great laboratories were built for this purpose, one alone which employed more than 3900 scientists and others, and solemn warnings have been issued by such men as Dr. Theodor Rosebury and Dr. Brock Chisholm that these subtler weapons may be even more devastating in their effects than atomic bombs. Friends have a testimony against war, and it is impossible to think of a Friend prostituting his knowledge in this way. But might it not be right to study this subject in order to discover means of defense against biological warfare as used by others? Here, perhaps, the issue is not so clear-cut; but several questions of principle arise on which Friends might be expected to have clear views. These have been expressed very forcibly by a non-Friend, Professor A. Charlotte Ruys, who was herself faced by the problem as a bacteriologist, living in an occupied country during the last war at a time when sabotage was regarded as a patriotic duty:

First, would one be free to publish results? War strategy might be opposed to it. And has any one the right to keep secret a means of defense against an infectious disease? Each scientist works on the vast basis of knowledge gathered by his predecessors. His new findings are only partly his own; they belong to all those whose work he has used. Therefore, secrecy is to be condemned. No scientist has the right to keep his findings for himself, his country, or the group to which he belongs.

To this verdict Friends, the "Publishers of Truth," might be expected to subscribe strongly. Professor Ruys goes on . . .

But the study of defense against a possible bacteriological war attack can never limit itself to defense against natural diseases. To be effective, the scientist will have to study the offensive side, with all the consequences it involves.

In order to obtain knowledge of the defense he will have to study thoroughly how the offensive forces of certain germs can be increased, how the resistance of the individual can be lowered, how defensive measures can be made useless by the enemy.

Such a study is like a poison which infiltrates the best thoughts of man.

And if one should find an extremely active offensive weapon would it be possible to keep it secret? It might be a very effective protection because it would prevent the enemy from attacking? So there is only one solution; no bacteriologist should take this line of work.

With that conclusion Friends generally would wholeheartedly agree.

Since, however, almost any development in science involves the possibility of wrong use, ought science to be studied at all? This question has arisen acutely in connection with the development of atomic and nuclear physics, and its prostitution to the making of atomic and hydrogen bombs and other atomic weapons. The developments in this particular field have undoubtedly owed much to the work of the Quaker scientist, John Dalton (1766–1844), who may fairly be regarded as the father of the modern theories of atomic structure and chemical combination, although the discontinuous nature of matter was a conception belonging to the period of Greek science.

Would it have been better if John Dalton and his contemporaries had not indulged in this kind of theoretical speculation; if Faraday and Henry had conducted no experiments on electromagnetism; if the technical and scientific developments of the nineteenth and twentieth centuries had remained unknown and if the world had remained, say, in the days of sailing vessels, stagecoaches, and tallow candles? Should science now call a halt to new discovery and wait until the world is once more fit to be trusted with dangerous knowledge? Matches are useful things, but we do not give them to babies to play with; is not mankind in its ethical infancy? Babies, however, cannot be prevented from experimentation. It is the way in which their intelligence grows. As long as children want to know what makes the wheels go round there will always be some who will try to improve the mechanism. The desire for knowledge is too fundamental a part of man's make-up to be suppressed, and Friends have never felt that the disinterested search after scientific truth is, or could be, a wrongful pursuit. The risk that knowledge, when found, may be wrongfully applied is one that must be taken not only in connection with science, as such, but in every branch of human activity.

Two points in particular must, however, be stressed. The first is that since the findings of science may be so grievously misused, Quaker scientists, and indeed Quakers in general, will feel a strong personal responsibility, as citizens, to ensure that they are not so misused. The second is that no Quaker would deliberately seek knowledge in order to put it to wrong use, and this may well mean that certain avenues of investigation are closed. In this, of course, Friends are not alone. To take one outstanding example: the results of certain human experiments in the Nazi concentration camps were deliberately destroyed when found, because it was generally felt, among decent people, that this kind of experiment ought not to have been undertaken. Friends would also, I think, feel the greatest sympathy with Sir Walter Moberly in the protests he makes, in *The Crisis in the University,* of all experiments or applications of science in which man takes to himself the attributes of God and attempts to shape other men to a mold of his own choosing. Which among us is fit for such a responsibility?

In Dr. Schrodinger's recent book, *Science and Humanism*, he begins by asking whether the promotion of knowledge within a narrow domain has any value in itself. Or whether even the sum total of the achievements of all the sciences together has any value, and if so what value? He rejects the obvious answer that would point to the practical consequences of scientific inquiry in transforming technology, industry, engineering (although this is the only value that Tolstoi would have admitted, and *that* only insofar as the benefits were shared by the common man), and he argues that natural science is a branch of pure learning, supporting this by pointing to those sciences, such as cosmology, which have no obviously *practical* bearing at all on the life of human society but which are valued no less than physics or chemistry in the eyes of scientists themselves.

Friends have long been interested in science simply as a subject of study which perhaps they might have rationalized in earlier days, or even now, by referring to the necessity of understanding the ways of the Creator, but which was and is primarily the natural activity of an inquiring mind, or the frank and proper enjoyment of nature, observation, calculation, or philosophy. The Society of Friends has abounded in botanists, geologists, and astronomers. Indeed, it has been pointed out that while Friends have limited the forms of recreation that were felt to be worth while, the study of natural history has always taken a high place among permissible leisure-time occupations, as it has in education at Quaker schools.

The Natural History Society at Bootham School, England, founded in 1834, was the first school society of its kind in Europe. In these days of much leisure and of too much mechanical recreation, the value of such pursuits might well be stressed more highly. But it was hardly likely that the practical value of these studies should be overlooked by such practical people. George Fox, in proposing the formation of schools for boys and girls, suggested that among other things "civil and useful in the creation" they should be taught "the nature of herbs, roots, plants and trees"; and he himself left some land in Philadelphia, sold to him for twenty-five pounds by William Penn, part of which was to be enclosed "for a garden, and to plant it with all sorts of physical plants for lads and lasses to learn simples there, and the uses to convert them to—distilled waters, oils, ointments, etc." It is not surprising, therefore, that early Friends included among their number several families of apothecaries, who were both pharmacists and general practitioners in country districts and helped to train other Friends, such as John Fothergill and William Allen, who became notable physicians and scientists in their turn. The history of some of these families and of their industrious apprentices is given in Arthur Raistrick's *Quakers in Science and Industry* (1950).

The travels of the early Quakers, both in the publishing of truth, in the search for religious freedom, and in the interests of commerce, brought them into foreign places which had a natural history different from that of their home country. It is interestingly typical of Quaker horticulturalists and botanists that they were all concerned to introduce to Great Britain seeds, plants, and trees from abroad and also special methods of cultivation. The Dr. John Fothergill grew more than three thousand tropical species in his hothouses and sent collectors to North America and West Africa for specimens. It is recorded that he refused to take a fee for his services from one of his patients who was a sea captain, but asked instead for two barrels of earth from Borneo. When it came, he was rewarded by the appearance of many strange plants from this foreign soil. John Collinson (1693–1768), a contemporary and a friend of John Fothergill's, although by trade a wholesale woolen draper and a very conscientious and successful one too, was by inclination a botanist. He was responsible for the importation into Great Britain of many plants from America, and he planted one thousand cedars of Lebanon in Goodwood Park. For thirty years a member of the Council of the Royal Society, he acted as a link between men of science in all parts of the world. He introduced their discoveries to the Royal Society and to each other, and it was he who stimulated his friend Benjamin Franklin to carry out the electrical experiments for which his name is honored.

This point is stressed because it is clear that the international character of scientific investigation is one that must not only commend itself to Friends, but that they themselves have helped to establish. Thomas Hodgkin, a Quaker physician of the first half of the nineteenth century, wrote: "The temple of Science is erected on a neutral territory, to which no age, and no nation, can lay a peculiar claim." Today the fabric of science is one to which barriers against free international communication are peculiarly damaging, and in which secrecy acts as a dry rot, no less harmful because its ravages are not so quickly seen. In urging the eradication of these evils, Friends base their objections to them on fundamental principles. It is not scientists themselves who are responsible for these barriers; scientists are, by their very habits of thought, free (in the main) from personal or national jealousies and rivalries and would subscribe wholeheartedly to Article Nineteen of the Declaration of Human Rights:

Everyone has the right to freedom of opinion and expression; this right includes freedom to hold opinions without interference and to seek, receive, and impart information and ideas through any medium and regardless of frontiers.

Paradoxically enough, however, it is the advance of science, and in particular its application to the art of waging war, that has led to the present schizophrenic attitude of many scientists. During the Napoleonic War, Sir Humphry Davy accepted a prize and a medal from Napoleon for his scientific discoveries and when criticized, as of course he was, replied simply, "Nations or countries may be at war, but men of science are not. That would indeed be civil war of the worst description." Later, while the war was still in progress, he traveled unmolested through France on a scientific journey. That would be impossible today. Not merely war, but the very threat or possibility of war can cause scientists in every country to abandon their traditions, to agree to secret work, to accept restrictions on travel and on the exchange of publications without protest, or with only the mildest of protests, even while, at the same time, they deplore the effects of these restrictions on science itself.

This is, of course, because they fear that a war in which their own country was *defeated* would bring even greater evils in its train for science, for the community of which they form a part, and for the ideals which they cherish.

Friends are aware of these dangers, but they believe that a man's ideals can be destroyed only by the weapon that he himself wields, that every war is a civil war, and that only a firm adherence to the principles of true internationalism based on a belief in the fatherhood of God and the brotherhood of man can bring about that reconciliation and freedom from fear which is the basis of a lasting peace. Quaker scientists in general cannot, therefore, agree to work under conditions of secrecy, and they must make every possible effort to remove those barriers which hinder full international co-operation. By so doing they believe that they most truly serve science, their own country, and mankind generally.

There are other aspects of the scientific method and of the scientific outlook which merit particular emphasis today, and which Friends would wish to see more widely applied. Many of the qualities that go to make a good scientist are indeed the qualities that make a good man of the world, a good world citizen, impervious to the art of the propagandist, the wiles of the charlatan, and the subtlety of the unscrupulous advertiser. The man of science must be wholly honest in observation and deduction. His integrity must be beyond reproach and his critical faculties highly developed. He must record his sense-impressions faithfully, because it is these, and these alone, that constitute his experimental data. It is by comparison with these data that he or other scientists will gradually decide which observations are reliable—that is, capable of repetition—and will deduce those relationships between sense-impressions (measurements or pointer-readings) that constitute physical laws. Unless his word can be relied upon, the value of his work is nil.

Quakers have always placed the highest emphasis on the necessity for strict truthfulness and it may well be, as H. G. Wood has said, that "there is a real connection between this dislike of the lie and the scientific impulse." Dr. Wood goes on to say: "I think it will be found that the ranks of scientific investigation have welcomed some of their ablest recruits from men who have been reared in this atmosphere."

The world would be a better place if this passion for truth were carried over, as a matter of course, into ordinary life, and it were regarded as unthinkably dishonest to distort news, to deceive by false propaganda, to make gratuitous assertions, or to repeat unconfirmed rumors as facts.

This does not mean that error has no place in scientific observation and deduction: on the contrary. The scientist knows, none better, that his observations can never be exact. He estimates his experimental error; and he even recognizes that besides the random errors inherent in his own fallibility or in the crudity of his apparatus, there may be systematic errors due to some factor that he has unintentionally overlooked. He must, therefore, be humble and admit that in spite of all his care he may be wrong, even within his own field. He must be willing to learn continually. He knows also (or ought to know!) that the scientific method of drawing inferences from observations, which consists essentially of framing and testing hypotheses until all are eliminated except those that fit the facts, is one that leads only to "high probability" and not to "absolute certainty."

The conclusions of the scientist will in any case be circumscribed by the state of existing experimental knowledge and by the mathematical tools at his disposal, as well as by the limitations of his own mind. He must expect that later generations of scientists will improve on his methods and will modify his conclusions, perhaps drastically. Nevertheless, within his own field and subject to the above limitations, he must stand by the results of measurements and deductions honestly made. He cannot allow the State or the Church or any other extra-scientific authority to dictate to him what he shall find in his own territory, or deny him the right to publish what he has found, if his only object in making the search was to find the truth. Nor can he allow himself to be inhibited in his search for truth by dogmatic metaphysical arguments or accusations, although the fact that he is a member of a human society may and indeed must prohibit the carrying-out of experiments dangerous to the well-being of that society. There is, of course, a paradox here, but it is a paradox of the kind that is always involved in the problem of freedom and responsibility within a community, and it emphasizes the point, to be made later, that science is not the whole of experience.

It was this refusal to be bound by the claims of dogmatic religion that led to clashes between scientists and churchmen from the seventeenth century onwards. The Royal Society itself was violently attacked as a conspiracy to undermine both society and religion; and the echoes of the disputes that raged around Huxley and Darwin are still reverberating in some of the communities dominated by fundamentalist mentality. On the whole, Quakers have been unaffected by this battle, because Quakerism is itself an experimental faith—that is, a faith rooted in experience and not founded on the dogmatic authority either of a book or of a priesthood. It must be admitted, however, that there was a period when the Society of Friends tended to "orthodoxy," and a number of Quaker scientists and medical men were "disowned" for unorthodox views that would now be regarded as merely liberal.

Dogmatism, both in politics and in religion, is frequently a sign of weakness, of unwillingness to face the opposition of heretics; or it may sometimes be a matter of prestige, a fear of appearing weak by admitting the possibility of having been mistaken; or a refusal to accept the responsibility of thinking. Dogmatism has expressed itself in the formulation of creeds; and religious creeds, as the Quaker astronomer Sir Arthur Eddington has said, "are a great obstacle to any full sympathy between the outlook of the scientist and the outlook which religion is so often supposed to require." He goes on to add, "I think it may be said that Quakerism in dispensing with creeds holds out a hand to the scientist." The scientific objection is not merely to particular creeds which assert in outworn phraseology beliefs which are either no longer held or no longer convey inspiration to life. The spirit of seeking which animates us refuses to regard any kind of creed as its goal.

It would be a shock to come across a university where it was the practice of the students to recite adherence to Newton's laws of motion, to Maxwell's equations, and to the electromagnetic theory of light. We should not deplore it the less if our own pet theory happened to be included, or if the list were brought up-to-date every few years. We should say that the students cannot possibly realize the intention of the scientific training if they are taught to look on these results as things to be recited and subscribed to. Science may fall short of its ideal, and although the peril scarcely takes this extreme form, it is not always easy, particularly in popular science, to maintain our stand against creed and dogma. I would not be sorry to borrow for our scientific pronouncements the passage prefixed to the Advices of the Society of Friends in 1656 and repeated in the current General Advices:

These things we do not lay upon you as a rule or form to walk by; but that all with a measure of the light, which is pure and holy, may be guided; and so in the light walking and abiding, these things may be fulfilled in the Spirit, not in the letter; for the letter killeth, but the Spirit giveth life.

This reminder that science must never become a creed is more necessary today than ever before, because there are those who believe in scientific measurement but believe that all else is meaningless; and others for whom science, in spite of (or because of!) its evolutionary character, is extrapolated to be a closed and dogmatic system capable of accounting for the whole of experience. Quakers are not likely to succumb to the dangers either of logical positivism or of materialism. The argument that because automatic machines can be constructed that will play games of noughts and crosses or even chess, against a human opponent, therefore the brain is nothing but a very complicated machine apart from which mind does not exist, is one that will leave their faith unshaken.

In *The Nature of the Physical World,* Eddington has dealt with some of these fallacies from the point of view of a Quaker scientist, but Friends base their beliefs essentially on personal experience rather than on rational argument although the latter is not avoided. They believe that God does reveal himself directly to man's consciousness, even though that which is not measurable cannot be defined. While willing to admit the autocracy of the scientific method within its own domain, they believe that domain to be limited. The scientist is going beyond his own mandate if he implies that what is outside his understanding has no significance; he is then indeed dogmatizing in the field of metaphysics. Even if the psychologist and the physicist between them should one day succeed in registering emotion on a machine and measuring it exactly as a weight or a length can be measured (and we are not, as scientists, too certain of what we mean even by such measurements), they would still know nothing of the actual emotion unless they had themselves actually experienced it.

Friends believe that in their direct contact with God they have such an experience which is beyond measurement and therefore outside the proper scope of science; as much outside it as seeing would be outside the scope of a man born without eyes. This difference is, as D. Elton Trueblood has said, that congenital blindness does not occur in the life of the Spirit. They know, of course, that in expressing this experience in words, even to themselves, they are bound to make use of the machinery of the brain and to formulate postulates which cannot be proved by the normal methods of the scientist. They know, indeed, that the individual's response to the seed of God within him may be conditioned by his environment, his previous history, and his state of health, mental and physical. It must be difficult, for example, to love your neighbor as yourself when you are starving and your neighbor has more than enough for his needs. So, in the same way, a man may *have* sight, and yet his capacity to see, to appreciate what he sees, or to describe what he sees may depend upon factors outside his optic system.

Friends admit that their belief that the God of their experience is the God expressed in the teaching, life, and death of Jesus Christ nearly 2,000 years ago, and their acceptance of this same Christ as ever-living, are axiomatic; they are the basis of their way of life, and are logically unprovable except in the sense that experience brings convictions. They are sure, as Eddington has put it, without being cocksure. But they are therefore all the more ready to realize what is not always realized by those to whom science is all-sufficient—that science is also based on axioms which are essentially unprovable except in the sense that experience brings conviction of "rightness" or "wrongness."

Friends, therefore, were not likely to make the mistake of supposing that the theory of determinism in the world of physics was a fatal blow at the doctrine of free will. Nor was the subsequent abandonment of that theory or the recognition of the essential discontinuity of physical events the occasion for the triumphant remark "I told you so." Friends who were physicists could accept the laws of both determinacy and indeterminacy for what they were, proper stages in the development of physical knowledge, without feeling the necessity for opposing or denying them either on grounds of theology or of common sense. They simply represented the results of observation within a closed field which was part, but not the whole, of experience.

This perhaps sums up Friends' approach to science. Science is an essential part of knowledge, in the forwarding of which Friends by their very training and outlook are well fitted to participate; but it is not capable of describing the whole of human experience, or of answering the questions: Who am I? Who are you? and Why are we here? Nor must science ever be allowed to become our God, any more than it should be made a scapegoat for our own shortcomings. Its proper place in the world today is that of a handmaid; we ourselves are responsible for seeing to it that it is rightly used.

Health and Healing
BY
HOWARD E. COLLIER

XI

Health and Healing

BY

HOWARD E. COLLIER

M.D., presently engaged in Industrial Medicine in England. Formerly, head of department of Industrial Medicine in a British university, and general practitioner for forty years.

Two simple but profound insights lie at the heart of Quakerism and produce the special characteristics of the typical Quaker approach to my problem, namely: the affirmation of the unity of all life experience; and the affirmation that the experimental way is the only royal road to a knowledge of truth, right, and conduct. To the Quaker, the distinctions between natural and supernatural, secular and sacred, are differences of quality and of degree, and are not absolute differences of kind or nature.

When these two insights are combined, the Quaker approach becomes inevitable. He carries his experimental method into his religious life and uses it to solve both spiritual and mundane perplexities. This point seems to be so essential to a true understanding of all that follows that I make no apology for discussing it in some detail.

Modern civilization and modern technology have been founded—for good or ill—upon the experimental method. That method appeals directly to observation, and repudiates mere speculation and the appeal beyond experience to any external authorities whose pronouncements are incapable of being submitted to the tests of experience.

When Francis Bacon and the natural philosophers used the

experimental method for the first time, they restricted its use strictly to the study of nature and of natural man. They accepted the view, then current, that an absolute gap—or hiatus—existed between the natural and the "supernatural." When the Royal Society was founded soon after the Restoration of Charles II, its members agreed with Bishop Spratt, who explicitly laid it down that the experimental method should be applied only, and solely, to the study of natural phenomena. Spratt affirmed that the natural philosopher was free to wander at his will among the natural powers, excluding only the soul and God. These last were to be reserved as the distinct and separate province of supernatural philosophers or theologians. In other words, they assumed that there was a basic and "incurable" duality in life; and made "absolute distinctions" between natural and supernatural Truth. Needless to say, this rigid scheme soon broke down in practice. Neither the soul nor God would consent to be banished from science or from experience. Almost all subsequent conflicts between science and religion seem to have stemmed from this root.

It was left to George Fox and the early Quakers, indirectly influenced, in my opinion, by the writings of Jacob Boehme and Paracelsus, to reject this false approach. Early Friends affirmed the "unity of the whole Creation." They denied the absoluteness of the distinction between sacred and secular and declared that experience—and in particular the experience of the "leading of the Inward Light of Christ"—was the method and touchstone by which both spiritual and mundane truths might be found and validated. This wholehearted acceptance of the experimental method seems to me to be the unique contribution made to modern civilization by the early Quakers and the distinctive element in the Quaker approach to contemporary problems.

One common misunderstanding of the Quaker method needs to be cleared up. The Quaker experimental method is not quite the same as the scientific method—at least as the scientific method is often misunderstood. A simple story will make this difference obvious. When Dr. Jenner, the discoverer of vaccination, consulted his friend John Hunter upon a certain difficulty, Hunter replied: "Don't speculate, but try the experiment." If this advice be uncritically accepted, the experimental or scientific method becomes degraded into little more than a machine for grinding out more and more facts. The Quaker would say that while it is right to avoid mere speculation, there are no valid grounds for supposing that a discovery of the facts will, of necessity, lead to a discovery of Truth. Only too often enthusiastic followers of the scientific method have thrown away the baby with the bath water. In rejecting mere speculation they have failed to realize the need for controlled reflection upon the facts, if truth is to be learned. In some hands the scientific method has only produced undigested masses of more or less unrelated facts, and often modern science has become a scientific technique which lacks both a sound theory and a coherent philosophy. What we need from modern science is to learn the true pattern and the right ordering of existing knowledge.

Insofar as this is a fair criticism of the modern scientific method, the Quaker will have none of it. The main points at issue are important. The Quaker insists that at all levels of experience truth can be found only by those who seek both to learn and to interpret the facts and do so, moreover, in a spirit of true worship and in reference to a set of true values. The Quaker insists upon a point overlooked by some of our scientists: namely, that problems that are studied in a physical setting can only warrant conclusions that are applied to physical events. In the search for Truth, the frame of reference in relation to which any matter is experimentally studied must be at least as wide and as comprehensive as the subject matter of the experiment.

While it is justifiable to seek to learn the physical truth about a physical body by studying it experimentally in a physical frame of reference, it is folly to try to study living organisms only in a physical frame of reference. Equally, it is folly and delusion to transfer results obtained from the study of the abstract sciences to the humane sciences and human behavior.

The problems of health and healing are problems of life and death; hence anyone who proposes to follow the Quaker approach into the study of health must study them in a frame of reference that is at least as wide as life. This is only another way of saying that the Quaker physician realizes that his problems in clinical medicine and hygiene ought to be studied both practically and reflectively. He must try to set his clinical problems against an eternal frame of reference and in the sight of God, who is the Whole. To the Quaker doctor, health consists in "living an Eternal life in the midst of Time," and, moreover, of living that life as a single, harmonized experience. Work and worship, reflection and experiment, make up the unity of life and are the two halves of the Quaker approach to all health problems.

One further point also needs particular emphasis. It is difficult to avoid the distorting influence of passion, prejudice, and self-interest in the conduct of the experimental method. Scientists escape this difficulty by "abolishing the soul and God" from their carefully arranged experiments. Clinical medical problems cannot be arranged and are seldom neat and tidy. In the Quaker view and according to Quaker experience, passion, prejudice, and self-interest can only be discounted by "controlled reflection in the Light of Christ"; that is to say, by worship.

The basis of scientific integrity is disinterestedness and the basis of the successful employment of the Quaker method is a positive concern for Truth—for Truth at all costs and in all places. Quaker integrity, wherever it exists, springs from worship as surely as scientific integrity springs from disinterestedness. If this point had been more generally realized in the past, modern science might not have been so frequently prostituted to serve vile purposes.

Insofar as the scientists—insofar as the Quakers—can escape from passion and self-interest, they become fitted to become interpreters of new truth as well as discoverers of new facts. In medicine the same principle applies. Sound clinical judgment depends more upon the doctor's ability to reflect and to interpret than it does upon the actual number and extent of the years of his practical experience. Without worship, Truth cannot be known either in medical practice or in life.

I was not born a Quaker. How, then, did I come to adopt the Quaker attitude? I was trained in scientific medicine and accepted the experimental method as the only means of discovering new knowledge about health and disease. It is by following that method faithfully that I became a Quaker and began to adopt the Quaker variant of the experimental method about which I have been writing.

At the end of the first world war I entered general practice, supposing that my work would be to apply scientific medicine to the cure of disease. I soon began to realize how inadequate and insufficient my scientific tools were to the tasks which they were expected to perform. In the homes of the poor and in my consulting room, I met human and not scientific problems. While I was walking the wards of the university hospitals I saw selected cases which were, in general, capable of scientific diagnosis. In private practice, the people who consulted me seemed to fall into no scientific category. They inhabited those vague borderlands that separate health from illness, or their manifest physical illnesses were reinforced and aggravated by fears, anxieties in the absence of morale and the will to get better. Many of them did not know what is was to be really well; some of them had never been adequately fed, housed, or clothed since the day they were born. Moreover, every individual's reaction to illness differed from that of his neighbor.

On rare occasions I came across a typical case of disease, but for the most part it seemed to me that I was called upon to practice what I had never been taught and that I had not been taught what I was called upon to practice. For example, no one instructed me in the art of seeing the person as a whole. I had supposed people needed to have their diseases cured, whereas I found that people really needed to be made whole. (And what, I asked myself, did I understand by being made whole?) It seemed to me that a whole person would be at one with his fellows, with his natural environment and, I supposed, in some sense at one with life and with God.

On such a view I felt that I ought to expect that such imponderable factors as the will-to-health, high morale of faith and hope, would be intimately connected with the healing of sick persons. Nor was there lack of positive and clear evidence in my practice to support this conception of health. What was I to make, for example, of the astonishing differences in the ways in which different people faced, responded to, the challenge of serious illness—or failed to do so, as the case might be? Some people seemed to wilt under trivial illness; others, refusing to be beaten, survived the severest illnesses or operations. Perhaps the difference lay in a constitution; but then, I asked myself, how explain many cases of unexpected recovery in constitutionally enfeebled persons, and especially among those who were surrounded by the love and the prayers of their friends and relations? Science suggested that such facts as these were irrelevant. Believe me, they are not irrelevant in private practice, where everything may seem to turn upon the faith of a mother or upon the loving care of a daughter for her sick parent. Coincidence and chance could also be summoned to explain these anomalies, but after a few years of experience the family doctor begins to feel that the long arm of coincidence is being unduly stretched and that explanation by the laws of chance is not satisfactory.

It was equally obvious that these imponderable influences in healing could not always be attributed to the practice of religion as such, since there was no evidence of their presence in many people who professed to be religious. On the contrary, such people were often hag-ridden by fear and showed by their low morale that they were not wholesome people.

Furthermore, at that time faith healing and Christian Science were being actively practiced by some of my patients. A sad series of avoidable tragedies—avoidable, I mean, by the ordinary standards of physical medicine—occurred in my own practice. Parents were robbed of their children, wives of their husbands, and young people of their ability to earn their living. It seemed, therefore, that if the influences that make for healing were, in fact, religious in nature, some religions must be judged to be more wholesome than others!

The same period witnessed the rise of modern analytic psychotherapy, which offered an additional means of diagnosis and healing and claimed to possess a thoroughly scientific discipline. As to this latter claim, opinions differed. In my own practice, psychoanalysis suffered from two serious disadvantages at that time. In the first place, it demanded more time and money than the majority of my patients could give to it; and in the second, it seemed to offer little more than a diagnosis of the emotional causes of certain states of ill health. Those of my own patients who underwent analysis returned to me in much the same state as they had left me. The fault may well have been their own. They said, rather sadly, that although they now knew the causes of their illness, that knowledge had not healed them. They had been analyzed, but not, it seemed, synthesized; they had been diagnosed, but not made whole. Curiously enough, it was just those people who lacked morale, drive, and the will-to-health who fell the victims of their own complexes. They seemed to lack some vital urge or incentive that would enable them to face and overcome the real difficulties with which they were beset.

I am ready to admit that my early experiences of the use of psychoanalysis may have been unfortunate and that many of its modern practitioners have learned much from their study of healthy minds and of genuine religious experience. Some of them have discovered where the "power-that-heals" operates in the human personality and how it may be released into human experience. The plain fact was, however, that those of my patients who were treated by analysis at that time were unable to make the vital leap that separates insight into causes of illness from the ability to do what is required for a cure.

At the same time, we must acknowledge our debt to the pioneers of medical psychology and also to Christian Science and the Faith Healers. Between them, they succeeded in opening the blind eyes of some of the members of the profession. They opened those eyes to the existence of powers and influences that operate through and reside in the mind and spirit of men. They opened my eyes to the possibility that faith, prayer, and worship might heal, even when all else seemed to have failed.

Several years of study and experiment followed. I became satisfied that what I called the religious or spiritual influences were important elements in all forms of healing, and that by their nature they slipped through the scientific sieve and were impossible to be made the subjects of a controlled experiment or of being scientifically measured or assessed. They were so elusive, it seemed, because they were personal and individual and varied from person to person.

It was at this period of my life, about twenty-five years ago, that I came in contact with the British Guild of Health, one of whose avowed objects was to increase co-operation between doctors and clergy in the cure of the sick and the establishment of health. The evidence which I gathered from this source soon convinced me that I was on the right lines in my experiments. At about the same time I fell seriously ill and, therefore, was able to make a first-hand trial of these practices and theories. Here I need only say that at that time and ever since I have found that the experience of the Guild of Health has been confirmed in my own experience.

The next step in my approach to these problems of healing was to wonder how I could reconcile and blend together the practice of religious healing with my practice of psychological and physical healing. Hitherto, I had been content to add psychology to physical medicine, as if they were more or less independent systems of diagnosis and treatment. At this point in my life, I came into contact with the Religious Society of Friends. This covered in its life and witness all that I have tried to describe in the introduction to this paper.

Reading Quaker literature, and especially the *Journal* of George Fox, I found in it a psychology that seemed to me to match the best of the modern teachers. In the Meeting for Worship I was able to obtain the opportunities that I needed for sustained reflection. Moreover, in the day-to-day practice of the Quaker religion, I came into living touch with a source of power or morale that was strong enough to enable me not only to progress towards my own healing but also to persevere upon the experimental way. Nor was I alone in these discoveries. I felt that I could say with Robert Barclay (*Apology*): "In the Silent Assemblies of God's People I found the evil in me weakening, and the good raised up."

Of all the things that I have since learned from my contact with Quakerism, one thing stands out. The healing influences and powers reside neither in the doctor, nor in his medicines, nor in surgical operations. Doctors may cure diseases; medicines and operations may remove the hindrances that are preventing healing; but only the *Vis Medicatrix Naturae*—or, as I should say, the healing powers of God—alone make men whole. As Ambroise Paré once said: "I dressed his wound; but God healed him." No one who has not learned this ancient truth can ever become a healer.

Aided by the two basic Quaker insights—the unity of life and the universal validity of the experimental method in the search for Truth—I began to take a new and heightened interest in my medical work and to examine my theory and my practice from a new angle. I had regarded illness as being due, for all practical purposes, either to some physical or some mental cause. Why should not all illnesses of all kinds be due to both of these, and, perhaps, to a third unnoticed group of influences? Only those who have escaped from the tyranny of the *either-or* will realize the emancipation of thought, since quite obviously the treatment of illness ought not to be *either* physical *or* psychological, but *both* of these; *and* spiritual, or religious, as well. Positive health also was now seen as a "living concert of three viols." Naturally many perplexities remained, some of which are still incompletely resolved.

My chief difficulty was to learn how to distinguish the lines of separation between body and mind, or the flesh and the spirit. In general terms the distinctions are clear enough for practical purposes. For example, the finite-mental nature of the mental element within a reflex arc (e.g., the blinking reflex) was obviously different in quality and perhaps was different in kind, from the so-called mental events associated with an experience of the beautiful; a feeling of having faith was obviously different from the feeling that two and two make four; reflection and intuition seemed markedly different from the processes called logical reasoning and deduction, and so on. Nevertheless, I found it hard to define these differences.

Aided by A. N. Whitehead, *Science and the Modern World*, and Charles Sherrington, *Man on His Nature*, I found two or three criteria which seemed adequate for my practical needs.

First, experiences which we call *valuing* or *giving* were predominantly spiritual, as distinct from mental; awareness was an awareness of unity, rather than of diversity. Spiritual awareness is a unitative state; whereas mental awareness is associated with attending to discrete things, ideas, acts, or events. And lastly, spiritual activity is carried out in a different frame of reference from that in which mental life is lived. The frame of reference in which all spiritual experience is consciously or unconsciously carried out transcends time and space and belongs to the eternal aspect of human experience. The finite mind operates in the reference-frame of time and space. This last criterion I owed to Sherrington, who distinguishes explicitly the finite mind from the non-finite and eternal mind, or spirit.

It is almost unnecessary to qualify this point by saying that in life as it is lived all of these three categories or qualities of experience (the bodily, the mental, and the spiritual) are intimately blended together and interfused to make one whole. But they are sufficiently distinct for practical clinical purposes, and as abstractions they are useful for the analysis of experience and for the treatment of illness. In any event we must make use of some abstractions. It seemed to me both sensible and reasonable to abandon the false "body-mind abstraction," which had only led me into a clinical muddle, and to adopt this triple analysis of experience which at the least seemed able to take all, and not only some, of the facts into consideration and account.

In practice this new approach worked out with simplicity and smoothness. Let us suppose for example that I was treating a patient who was suffering from some heart disorder. I asked myself firstly whether drugs, graduated exercise, or rest would enhance the efficiency of his heart muscle and circulation. If so, they must be prescribed. Turning next to the condition of his finite mind—and the passions of the flesh—I considered whether there were fears, obsessions, anxieties, or dreads that were lowering his heart-efficiency or preventing him from making maximum use of the remaining powers of his heart. Psychotherapy might help here. But to stop at this point was to fail to make a complete diagnosis. What about his values and attitudes; what was the meaning of life for him? The word *attitude* best describes this line of clinical approach. What has religious healing to offer to this patient and how can he be helped to obtain religious healing and a better attitude toward life and himself? Obviously this is a very delicate question, and one which only a fool would pose to his patient in a blustering way. It is a query which an angel would but whisper. Nevertheless, the treatment of a sick person cannot be said to be complete until this query has been asked and answered by the patient.

I have never stopped to ask myself whether patients, like the one mentioned above, were cured by digitalis, by psychology, or by religious healing. Such a question is silly and unprofitable and, in the majority of instances, unanswerable. All that matters is that by the complete treatment people are always helped, and frequently made whole.

In trying to assess in my own mind the value and efficiency of the religious element in healing, two probable conclusions formed in my mind. It appears to me to be probable that there are certain natural limits to the ability of the flesh to respond to the influences of the eternal spirit. That, at least, is the conclusion to which my own experience and observation point. This conclusion differs from the expressed views of many religious healers and must be regarded as still undecided.

My own evidence suggests that recovery from such severe catastrophes as severed limbs and destroyed eyes never takes place, that the effects of advancing years and the natural degenerations that accompany old age in civilized communities are not removed by religious healing. Nevertheless, it is remarkable how completely a patient may recover from, or successfully adapt himself to, the effects of drastic surgery and destructive nervous disorders like poliomyelitis or hemiplegia, and from conditions often regarded as incurable.

The other conclusion was equally important. I have seen many a person made whole-in-spirit whose physical health remained far below normal for his age. As George Fox once said, "There be miracles in the spirit of which the world knows nothing."

I have always been careful to avoid making any promises to

my patients. We should never offer bodily health as if it could be won as a prize that will be awarded to those who reach the goal of faith. On the contrary, we are told, "Seek ye first the Kingdom," and that then whatever may be needful for us—so that we may continue to seek the Kingdom—will be "added unto us." It seems to me that we may be fully assured of so much help. Health is given to man, or health is restored, in order to serve, and never for self-gratification. But since the eternal spirit resides at the hub and center of the self, one should never despair of the possibility of healing. When the center of the self is made whole, its peripheral parts are apt to be restored also. That, at least, is my own experience; that is what I have observed.

Another valuable Quaker insight provided me with practical guidance on this point. As Quakers, we are enjoined always to try "to speak to the condition" of our hearers. We must speak Latin to the Romans and English to the English: we must not offer meat to babes nor milk to the mature! Provided I was careful to adapt my religious healing to what I discovered to be the spiritual state and spiritual age of my patient, I seldom failed to win an answering response. To the professedly irreligious, I have spoken of goodness, of truth and of beauty, or have enjoined them to "have faith in life, since it seldom lets us down"; or, at a still simpler level, I have asked people to "trust my judgment in this matter." Before all, I have tried to set out the ideal possibility that they might yet be healed if only they would attend as they should to the culture of the neglected aspects of their lives and personalities. Even at this simple level, religious healing can be remarkably effective; the more so since it often initiates a long process of spiritual growth in the person who accepts it; in other words a process of progressive healing. No one will understand the Quaker approach to illness who does not recognize that, in the Quaker view, God is "experienced in measure" by every man, and that there is "that of God in every man" to which a direct and confident appeal always may be made, provided the right word be said, in the right tone and at the right time. Even those who reject the religious appeal are ready to consider the ideal of personal integration: that is to say, the aim of becoming a whole person.

Some people will object that the busy doctor can have no time for such an elaborate approach to clinical problems as the one outlined above; others will object that to make this approach is to trespass on the domains of the clergy. If the doctor has no time to treat his patients, there must be something wrong with the organization of the medical services. As to the second objection, I do not question that the clergy are specially trained to deal with disordered souls, but as a member of a religious society in which there exists no special class of ministers, I have been bound to attempt what I could for those who came to me. A Quaker physician must always try to keep within the unity of life, and hence he must give such spiritual first-aid as may be within his powers and competence. Moreover, it is clear to me that personality healing properly belongs to the art of medicine, and personality healing necessarily involves religious healing. So much seems clear to me.

I soon realized that the complete diagnosis and treatment need not be confined to the sick. It applied equally to those who were in good health and it applied in the fields of social and industrial medicine. If I could show my patients the way to attain to the highest possible degrees of positive health attainable by them in their present state and age, I should not only make my own work easier but I should render a great service to mankind. Unfortunately, current health propaganda and current teaching in mental hygiene, valuable as they are, usually fail at the cardinal point. We all know, more or less exactly, what we ought to do to keep well; but do we do what we ought? Positive health clearly calls for discipline of body and of mind. It also calls most insistently for a true spiritual dedication of the self to some admittedly worthy end. Health education is not simple; what is needed is to point to the true success of health morale or drive. To seek for health as an end in itself is a sure way to miss it. The vital question which we need to ask is not, Am I fit? but, For what am I fit? Who can give me strength for that service?

Where can we find the worthy purpose, the high morale, the drive, the courage, and the self-denial that will make us ready to seek positive health in order that we may serve—not self— but others?

No argument is needed to show that in the final analysis the springs of positive health and the roots of preventive medicine are deeply buried in the life of the spirit and of religion. To me, at least, it is clear that there is no other source from which a sufficiency of steadily enduring motive and power can be derived. Therefore, the doctor must say to everyone that positive health requires the co-ordinated and balanced culture of body, mind, and spirit. Perhaps he will use simpler words than these, but at least he will mean as much. The results that follow this approach to the problems of preventive medicine still await full study and here lies a fruitful field for the use of the experimental method.

Some results are already apparent in the social as well as in the personal spheres of life. In factory, workshop, and office—wherever men and women work together—this triple diagnosis and treatment of their social disorders can be effectively applied. In modern industry a few heresies obstinately persist. There is the notion, for example, that "only the wage envelope speaks" and that if good wages are paid, nothing else matters. No one questions the primary need for adequate wages, for good conditions of work, and for avoiding any exposure of the workers to polluted or poisoned atmospheres, but it is far from being true that the positive health of the workers in our factories can be measured by the size of their wages or by the physical hygiene of the factory.

Health at work—to say nothing about efficiency and the level of production in a factory—depends much more than is often supposed upon whether the workers are regarded and treated as persons and upon the presence or absence of group harmony or contentment in the factory.

As an industrial doctor I have found it useful and helpful to apply the complete diagnosis to the problems of industrial health and illness. I have regarded the working group as if it were a patient, and have tried to apply the complete treatment to the group-life of the factories in which I have worked. It would carry me far afield to discuss this aspect of my medical work in detail. Suffice it to say, my experience has taught me that this line of approach opens up valuable means of industrial social healing and of the prevention and cure of unrest in industry.

Two other aspects of the Quaker approach to social healing seem worthy of note. One of the unique values of that approach is that it can always be employed in whatever situation of difficulty, illness, or conflict you may become involved. At the time of the great depression (1928–1934), almost all of my patients fell into unemployment. Whole streets of families were out of work. As an individual I was helpless and powerless to help in this situation. But the Quakers, as a group, set about the task of attempting to heal some of the evil consequences of this vast social catastrophe. In my home town some of my friends, not all of whom were Quakers, but all of whom were Christians, started local allotment schemes, an unemployed center and a craft school.

These schemes were valuable as first-aid measures at the time. They demonstrated, at least, our real concern for our fellows and they enabled a few men to find alternative means of earning their living. As the crisis slowly passed, our experiments were closed. But, and this is the significant point, the modern practice of rehabilitation or re-ablement, which is now conducted on a large scale, and officially, by the Ministry of Labour, owed its conception and its existence to these pioneer experiments which were made all over the country and were especially useful in South Wales and in Lancashire. It is not too much to say this powerful new means of social healing was first worked out through local small-scale attempts to apply the Quaker approach to healing in town, village, and great city.

It seems probable that we are now beginning to see the application of another important part of the total Quaker approach in another branch of medicine. As a doctor in ordinary practice, I have seen much evidence of the value of the silent Meeting for Worship as a method of healing illness of the emotional life and of the personality. I have been gathering this evidence during the last quarter of a century. It seems to me to be probable that lessons which Quakers have slowly learned concerning the conduct of the Quaker Meeting may soon be applied and used as a method of group-psychotherapy for many emotional ills and for the personality-illnesses.

Psychologists are inclined to agree that many emotional disorders can be traced back to faults in the love-life of those who suffer from them. They arise from faults in human relations and from difficulties in adjustment between the sick person and other people. Hence in essence these illnesses are as much social illnesses as they are personal illnesses. This being the case, is it likely that socially-determined illnesses will be successfully treated by any individual doctor—no matter how skillful? Emotional illnesses may be diagnosed in the consulting room, they can only be healed in community. The Quaker Meeting and the Quaker fellowship which develop from every live Meeting are ideally designed to provide this healing society in which the lonely, isolated, or morbidly shy individual may find both himself and his healing.

The recent remarkable growth of clinics for group-psychotherapy and their undoubted value as a means of psychological healing support my own experience. In my view the Quaker Meeting and the normal, healthy fellowship life which should surround it provide a powerful and hitherto neglected means of true social healing, at least in many cases.

There seems to me no reason why the techniques and principles worked out in the Meeting for Worship should not be modified and adapted to suit other classes of people provided, of course, it is not forgotten that it is the spirit of the Meeting and the spirit in the Meeting, and its technique of corporate silence alone, that provides its healing powers. Research is being conducted on these lines.

Hitherto I have written about a doctor's approach; I conclude by giving a brief account of the personal values which I have derived from my own acceptance of the Quaker method. A doctor's life is never an easy one, since it is physically arduous and emotionally exacting. I have derived certain negative and positive personal values from the Quaker way of life. Submission, resignation—the placid folding of the hands before the other person's difficulty—are foreign to the Quaker mind. A local experiment in healing can and must always be attempted in some small way. Nor can the Quaker shut his eyes to evil or pretend it is not there; only those people who dwell in suburbia can act as if slums did not exist. The Quaker attitude positively encourages us to try to enter into every situation of suffering or conflict: but to enter it as one who serves and suffers with the unfortunate and not as a teacher, still less as a preacher. Seeing both the evil and the good in every situation, the Quaker can preserve his faith and hope. As a doctor he knows that even if he is in the presence of an incurable illness, the eternal spirit of his patient may be made whole; his patient may be given peace and joy.

Furthermore the Quaker approach counsels patience and does not lead us to expect to discover the New Jerusalem around the next corner. The experimental method may be slow, but at least it is sure. Even if we see few results, yet others may reap where we have sown, or perhaps our small experiments may open up some new and better way of healing. As I have experienced this approach, the Quaker attitude provides the chief antidote to the poisons of indifference and despair. It is, in fact, the old alchemists' *elixir vitae*. Try the experiment and see what happens!

In the Meeting for Worship and in the life of private study and contemplation which is its counterpart, the weary, harassed doctor can find rest of body, relaxation of mind, and enhancement of his spiritual and emotional energies. I have discovered that it is one thing to make a good start on a long race and quite another to persevere in it, in spite of weariness and discouragement. We start out in our medical careers full of zeal and high ideals; before long we tend to become "only an embodied bedside manner"—mere automata, or charlatans!

Worship blended with action; action that leads us back to worship; these are the ways to be kept steady in the pursuit of our ideals and to be refreshed in spirit so that, ceasing to be mere doctors, we become, in our measure, healers of the sick. To my mind it is not a question whether a busy doctor can find time for worship and religion: the real questions are, how can anyone continue to heal who is not progressively being healed himself; how can one become whole without worship?

Finally, the greatest single positive value that is derived from following the Quaker approach is that it is always an approach from *within* and never from *without*. The parable of the "leaven which a woman took and hid in a barrel of meal until the whole was leavened," contains the heart and essence of the Quaker approach. I have already tried to show how the principle of the leaven can be applied to the major problems of personal and social healing. How does it apply to our own personal and individual search for positive health?

The acceptance of the Quaker approach launches us upon the greatest adventure of our lives: namely, the inward quest, during which we seek to find our true self—that hidden self whom the world never sees, whom we do not, at first, know—that hidden self who was born as a child of God and is destined to become a son of God in this life on earth. Here again the experimental method is the one and only road to true self-knowledge and self-understanding.

It would be a long tale to recount the full history of my own inward search. Suffice it to say here that every search ends in a finding. It is a finding not so much of myself as of my *self* and of Him who reveals Himself at last as The Inward Christ. In experience, at last and in our measure, we meet "The Christ, who desires to dwell in the narrow rooms of the house of Everyman." I am conscious of the gaps and the defects in my account of the Quaker approach to health and healing. These will be apparent not only to my professional colleagues but still more, perhaps, to my coreligionists. In his statement of the results of his experimental approaches to life, the Quaker is rightly enjoined to be careful never to exceed his own measure. I have tried to understate rather than to exaggerate. It seems to me that if the experimental way were consistently followed by doctors in the future, several consequences might confidently be expected. There would be a rapid increase in personal and social health; there would be a lessened incidence of most diseases, and a heightened efficiency-for-service, on all sides. But what seems to me to be much more important, there would be a great increase in the practice of a living religion. Our children could then see what we have prayed for: namely, the day when the original unity of Christ's healing and Christ's gospel will have been restored as it was in "The Days of His Flesh."

Present Secular Philosophies

BY

D. ELTON TRUEBLOOD

XII

Present Secular Philosophies

BY

D. ELTON TRUEBLOOD

Professor of Philosophy, Earlham College, formerly Professor at Haverford, Stanford, and Howard Universities; author of many books in the fields of Philosophy and Religion including The Predicament of Modern Man *and* The Life We Prize.

THE RELATIONSHIP of Quakerism to the secular thought forms of succeeding generations has been necessarily complex. This necessity arises from two facts: Quakerism, having no set creed, is particularly free to learn from any new thought as it emerges; and Quakerism rooted in certain basic experiences is able, at the same time, to resist the pressure of contemporary intellectual fashions. The Quaker way of life is thus neither a reflection of the changing intellectual pattern nor a fixed system, wholly independent of such patterns. Friends, since the outset, have resisted both an authoritarian position on the one hand, and directionless change on the other.

There have been periods, during the three centuries of Quaker history, when the Society of Friends has been an organization markedly separate from the world. This was particularly true in the eighteenth century, and in part of the nineteenth, but it was not at all true in the burst of life in the seventeenth century with which Quakerism began, and it has been increasingly untrue during most of the last hundred years.

In all the greatest periods, Friends have resisted the temptation to set themselves apart from the world.

Though Quakerism began as a great upsurge of religious experience, the leaders of the new movement soon realized that an intellectual formulation was a necessity, if the movement were to be more than transitory. Several able men, of the second generation of Friends, used their well-trained minds for this purpose and, accordingly, established the method of defense which the time required. The most successful of these men, William Penn and Robert Barclay, were keenly aware of the secular movements of thought in their generation. Barclay made abundant references to many authors, including one of the Cambridge Platonists, and felt the necessity of stating the new position in such a way that it would be acceptable to learned people conversant with the thought forms of his day. His *Theses*, which preceded his *Apology* and of which his well-known book is an elaboration, was addressed to the learned. This is why the *Apology* appeared in Latin before the author made an English translation. Even George Fox, who was not an educated man, evidently felt the impact of contemporary thought. Perhaps the best evidence of this is his use of the word *experimentally*, as when he wrote "And this I knew *experimentally*." Here was a reflection, possibly unconscious, of the beginning of the empirical tradition in British philosophy.

Modern Quakerism, especially in the last half century, has been deeply inspired by the conscious attempt to recover the vitality of seventeenth century Quakerism. Accordingly, it is not surprising that the openness to secular thought has again been marked. In the twentieth century Friends have numbered among their ranks several outstanding scientific thinkers, of whom the most notable was the late Sir Arthur Eddington, whose Gifford Lectures, *The Nature of the Physical World*, were widely read and honored on both sides of the Atlantic. Professor Eddington's specific Quaker application of his scientific philosophy appeared in his Swarthmore Lecture for 1929, called *Science and the Unseen World*.[1]

The leading Quaker philosopher of the last generation was Professor Rufus M. Jones, of Haverford College, who reached

---

1. *Swarthmore Lecture*, 1929. (London : George Allen & Unwin Ltd).

a wide audience through his many books and addresses. He represented a conscious effort to take advantage of secular thought without giving up, in any degree, the distinctive Quaker approach. His chief academic preparation came through graduate study at Harvard University when Harvard philosophers were world famous. Rufus Jones learned from all of them, but the greatest impact came from William James. His many books on mysticism appeared partly from the desire to fill a gap which James recognized but did not feel qualified to fill.

Insofar as contemporary Quaker thinkers are cognizant of the secular thinking of our day, they must reckon with the dominance of natural science. It is applied science, more than any other single factor, that has altered the externals of our life, and it is applied science that has made our historical crises both more dangerous and more pervasive of the entire human family. The result is that some people in our day practically worship at the shrine of science while others fear its destructive power. In the popular mind, science is a magic word, millions believing a doctrine if it is upheld by science, though doubting it on almost all other grounds. The critical are aware that science has made possible both our greatest material advance and our worst destruction. Atomic fission, with its amazing potentiality for both good and evil, becomes the most representative symbol of our complex age.

The basic Quaker attitude to science is necessarily a mixed one, once the nature of Quakerism is understood. On the one hand Friends have engaged very widely in scientific enterprises. The Quaker colleges have usually had strong scientific faculties, while a number of Friends have carried on private scientific research. We need only to mention such names as Dalton and Cope to realize how strong this Quaker scientific tradition is. Friends have believed that the world is God's world, in all its parts, and accordingly have thought they ought to try to understand it as carefully and accurately as is possible for the human mind to do. Scientific method is adopted because it is a method which increases our accuracy of observation and of inference.

Though some Friends in the past no doubt resisted the conclusions that existing species have evolved, by transformation, from other and earlier species, such resistance has not had anything to do with the central convictions of Quakerism. Since Friends held, all along, that there was something more basic than the Scriptures, however valuable the Scriptures were as confirmation, those who sought to be consistent Friends were not long or seriously worried by the apparent conflict between Genesis and geology or biology. If inspiration is immediate and potentially continuous, God has new truth to give to men, and we naturally sit down as little children before the fact, whatever the fact turns out to be. Partly for this reason Friends have experienced relatively little of the much publicized conflict between science and religion.

This friendliness to science has been even more marked in the ultimate basis of our theological thinking. It is a good part of the mood of science to seek to base conclusions upon experience rather than to make conclusions in advance of experience or independent of it. It is this mood which makes the consistent scientist the enemy of all prejudice. Quakerism is the most striking application of this mood to religion. Central to all of our religion, at least in the Judeo-Christian tradition, is belief in God as One who exists, independent of us and our knowing Him. But what reasons can we give for this belief? It is not enough to say that we are assured in our conviction, because the insane hospitals are full of persons who have unquestioned assurance of the most bizarre and contradictory beliefs. Because men and women can so easily be in error, even concerning those things about which they most deeply care, we must always find ways of looking for reliable evidence.

In support of belief in God there have been well-known arguments, especially those based on the conception of causation, of purpose, and of a moral order. It would be wrong to say, as some now do, that these are valueless, because each includes a kernel of truth; but it is accurate to say that they do not have wide appeal to the modern mind, insofar as it is influenced by scientific thought. Here is where the relationship between Quakerism and secular thought is particularly important. Quakerism, while neither denying nor minimizing the traditional theistic arguments, places the major emphasis on the evidence of direct experience. Friends have always held that the chief reason for believing in God is the same as the chief reason for believing in a tree, namely, the evidence of first-hand experience. If the dominant secular philosophy of our day is radical empiricism, Quakerism, more than any other Christian movement, is in the main stream of contemporary thought. This is an emphasis which might be expected to appeal to modern man, who tends to be impatient with involved deductions but can appreciate the strength of the witness who says, "I was there."

There is, of course, one important difference between much of the scientific empiricism of our day and Quakerism in that the former tends to stress only the experience which comes by the senses, whereas Friends have never seen any good reason for this limitation. Friends readily agree that they do not "see" God by the same method that they see a tree, for in the religious experience there is no involvement of an end-organ, whether visual, auditory, or tactual. The religious experience, if it is genuine, is an experience of immediate communication between the finite self and God, without the indirect methods which mark the use of the sensory mechanisms.

There are people who rule out in advance the possibility of immediate non-sensory experience of God, on the ground that such an experience is impossible, but in doing this they are disloyal to the scientific mentality which they are supposedly espousing. How do they know that immediate experience between the finite self and the infinite self is not possible? When we analyze the objection, we find that it is only a prejudice and no part of scientific method. The scientific method takes the experience as it appears, observes without prejudice the reports that men and women have made in their alleged experience of God, and then analyzes carefully to see what valid references can be made. It is conceivable that those who hold all direct religious experience to be delusory are correct, but this cannot be known in advance. The Quaker empiricism is a truly radical empiricism in that it begins with the reported experience and goes on from there, observing the datum open-mindedly.

If we are to be scientific, we cannot neglect the fact that millions of persons, representing many different traditions and different centuries, have claimed to know the Living God as intimately and as truly as they have known either their neighbors or physical objects. This is a tremendous claim, never to be taken lightly by any thoughtful person, because, if the claim is substantiated, it tells us the most important fact we can know about our world, the news that we are not alone in our striving. If the experience is genuine, we ought to find that out; but if it is false, we ought to try to dispel the delusion. If it is a false claim, we cannot avoid the further conclusion that many of those whom we have most reason to trust in this area have been deluded and this would include even Christ Himself. Indeed, if the claim is false, then everyone who has reported direct contact with God in prayer has been a deluded person. Anyone who undertakes to prove this is involved in a large enterprise, perhaps larger than he realizes. That some have been deluded is no doubt true, but what is the chance that *all* have been?

The whole of Quaker thought may be seen as a continuous effort to uphold this religious empiricism. The Quaker journals have provided much accumulated evidence, comparable to the laboratory reports in a science, and the whole of Quaker history has been seen as a progressive verification. Friends have realized that they had to meet many serious objections, including the psychological ones, but this has been done with honesty and care.

The refusal of Friends to limit their empirical witness to the deliverance of the senses shows vividly how critical Quaker thought is in its acceptance of current science. Certainly Friends reject scientism, whenever that means that no conclusion can be acceptable unless it can be tested in a physical laboratory. There are undoubtedly a good many who think that the only trustworthy evidence is the evidence of the test tube or of the slide rule. Friends tend to consider such a position naïve and oversimple. There must be much more to the world than our paltry systems can indicate or prove. Friends understand keenly that science and the technology which rests upon it can help or harm human life, depending completely on the moral factors involved. Insofar as science is concerned, there is no reason why those engaged in cancer research should not use their knowledge and skill to *spread* cancer rather than to diminish it. It is because of the wholly nonscientific presuppositions that such an evil use seems unthinkable. In short, Friends are very conscious both of the glory and of the limitations of science and have always been so.

It was a Quaker thinker, H. G. Wood, who pointed out, at the outset of the late war, that the deepest objections to Nazi atrocities were not scientific ones. Much had been said of a doctrine of pure race, and this, we were assured, was poor science, but Professor Wood showed vividly that it would have been wrong, even if it had been good science. Friends are quick to use scientific skill, as, for example, in the production of synthetic foods in order to feed our late enemies, but Friends understand that the reasons for feeding our late enemies are not scientific reasons. These reasons come from a deeper level of experience than that of the ordinary laboratory.

Friends have the combination of flexibility and stability mentioned earlier, because Quakerism is rooted more in an experience than in a creed. We find the experience of the Living God as revealed by Christ so self-verifying through the years that it seems to us to be the fulcrum by which all else may be lifted. We can change our language and our systems of interpretation, but this experience we do not change. Accordingly Friends are bound to reject some of the secular philosophies of our day or of any day, while we take some parts of others and reject some parts. Quakerism seeks not to be a new religion or a new philosophy, but Basic Christianity or Primitive Christianity Revived, to use Penn's famous phrase. We believe that God *is*, that He is personal, that He is accurately revealed in Jesus Christ, that Christ can be known now as truly as He was known by the disciples. Now the point is that such convictions are compatible with some systems and not with others. If some of the popular philosophies of our day are true, this Basic Christianity is false and no compromise is possible. It may be useful to consider the various characteristic secular emphases of our day in order to see the relation of each to Quaker life, thought, and experience.

Naturalism. A great many contemporary thinkers speak of themselves as upholders of philosophical naturalism. They are not naturalists in the sense that a biologist is, but rather because of their world view. The system is usually marked by both a positive and a negative emphasis. The positive emphasis is that of the effort to see all life as one, to hold that there is a system of natural laws so that no part of the world is arbitrary or erratic in its behavior. The contention is that the promotion of natural science is impossible unless such a system of natural law exists. The usual claim is that the naturalistic order includes the actions of minds as well as the actions of bodies.

The negative emphasis of naturalism is the denial of the existence of any supernatural order. Thus, if God is, He exists only in the sense of immanence. The ordinary naturalistic dictum is that God does not and cannot exist, in a transcendent sense. Accordingly, most philosophic naturalists disbelieve in God in any personal way, and if they use the characteristic religious terminology, mean by it merely the tendency toward order or value to be observed in the evolving world around us. A good example of the effort to keep the religious mood while discarding the idea of God as transcendent is the late John Dewey's Terry Lectures, *A Common Faith*. The God so understood, being merely a tendency or unconscious force, is not one to whom men can pray or with whom men can have communication.

The Quaker approach to such naturalism is very clear. Quakerism accepts the notion that ours is an orderly world and thus has much sympathy with the affirmative aspect of naturalism. Quakers never hold that there is any area beyond inquiry or outside the sphere of law. But Quakers do not see any reason to hold that all order is of the same type. There is, indeed, the mechanical order which we see in many physical objects, but this need not deny the existence of a purposive order, which demonstrates higher principles of organization. Indeed, it is our claim that this purposive order is already known, in our conscious experience of planning our creativity and that what we are, in part, God is wholly and completely.

The existence of a natural order need not, logically, imply the denial of a supernatural order and Friends believe that it is only in the light of such a supernatural order of Divine Purpose that the natural order makes sense. The chief reason for believing this to be true is the inability of the natural order to be self-explanatory in terms of its own principles. If the world is essentially one, as all naturalistic thinkers believe, there is no convincing reason why its unity may not arise from the divine creation. The higher can explain the lower, but the lower cannot explain the higher. Moreover, Friends are bound to hold that, insofar as naturalistic thinkers reject the personal nature of God, they are wrong. This is because the common experience which has made the Society of Friends a fellowship of verification has been so deeply personal. In short, Friends have far more sympathy with the naturalists in what they affirm than in what they deny.

Positivism. The positivistic way of thinking, which received its first conscious formulation at the hand of the French sociologist Auguste Comte, sets itself up as the only truly scientific attitude. Positive knowledge is knowledge by direct observation and experimentation, say the positivists, and this they contrast with all speculation. In the twentieth century the doctrine has been given a new twist by a group, originally active in Vienna but now influential throughout the western world, calling themselves Logical Positivists. Perhaps the strongest center of their influence today is the University of Chicago.

The uniting doctrine of all logical positivists is that statements are meaningless unless they can be verified by the methods of natural science. By this, they mean that statements are nonsense unless they can make a demonstrable difference in terms of the senses. In its popular form this conception is now termed "scientific philosophy" and the tendency is to feel supercilious toward all preceding philosophers, including the ones, like Plato and Kant, who are usually highly honored.

It is obvious that logical positivism is wholly incompatible with Quaker thought. If Quakers are right in their trust in direct religious experience the logical positivists are wrong. These positivists are forced by their system to hold, not that Quaker claims are false, but rather that Quaker claims are meaningless. To ask whether men can know God is as foolish, the contemporary positivist thinks, as to ask whether a right-angled triangle is moral. Accordingly, the Quaker approach to positivism must be one of searching analysis. The Quaker must ask the positivist how he knows, with such certainty, that there is no knowledge or meaningful discourse other than that of sense experience. Certainly, he does not know this by sense experience. If this is a mere faith, how is it supported? Friends have had to do battle in this fashion before and they may need to fight on this issue with vigor in the coming days.

Realism. The growth of various kinds of realism has been one of the chief gains of philosophic thought in the twentieth century. All realism has been a revolt against subjective idealism, which tends to suppose that being is dependent upon being known. On the whole, the realistic conviction that there are objects which exist prior to their being known and independent of being known has won the field. There was, we believe, a world before there were men to observe it. Thought appears in nature, not nature in thought.

The dominant realism of our day is called "critical realism," stressing the idea that, though independent objects exist, the presuppositions of the knower make a difference in the total experience. The cognitive datum is always a complex structure, influenced both objectively and subjectively. The modern thinker who has defended this epistemological dualism with the most persuasive power is Professor A. I. Lovejoy of Johns Hopkins University.

Insofar as Quakerism involves a theory of knowledge it accepts a realism of this type, but Friends are very careful to see to it that such realism does not mean materialism. The objective factor in knowledge may be a material object, and Friends believe in such objects, but it may also be another mind. Above all, Friends hold the realistic position in regard to the knowledge of God, affirming that God, as known, is far more than a subjective experience on our part. Friends do not confuse God with the Idea of God. We do not need to choose between a subjective and an objective conception of cognitive experience because *both* are ordinarily involved. To show that religious experience involves subjective factors is not, therefore, to make a damaging attack upon its trustworthiness, because we know upon analysis that all experiences have these factors. My only experience of a tree is, of course, the subjective experience in my own mind, but this is not to deny the existence of an objective tree to which my thought refers. Similarly, the experience of God is known internally, but the presence of subjective factors does not entail the denial of objective factors.

Pragmatism. The pragmatic philosophy as developed, particularly in America in the early years of the present century, has had wide vogue. The great names connected with Pragmatism include not only William James, who used the word as the title of a book, but many others, such as John Dewey who developed a different vocabulary. Beginning with the notion of practical results as a valid and important test of truth, William James allowed himself to go on to the extreme position that working is the very meaning of truth. This has sounded very sensible and practical to many readers, but reflection shows the idea to be full of ambiguities. Does "works" mean cash value, or material difference, or increased mental satisfaction or what? What about the successful lie? Is it true so long as it works? If so, does truth change when the consequences change? Does a proposition *begin* to be true when it begins to work in practice, but was not true before? Do our moral standards depend upon their success? If so, then the only meaning of honesty is good policy.

Such questions were so serious in the thought of Rufus Jones that, much as he revered the memory of his old teacher, he often said he was sorry that William James wrote his *Pragmatism*. The Quaker approach is to pay a good deal of attention to practical results, but to hold that a proposition works because it is true, not that it is true because it works. Furthermore, Friends hold that some propositions are true even though they have never yet been verified. The sense that truth is august, objective, and essentially unchanging is very deep in the Quaker way of life. Truth is one of the great Quaker words, some of the early Quaker missionaries being called the First Publishers of Truth, and Friends may be counted upon to resist any intellectual movement which detracts from the nobility of this conception.

This is particularly true in regard to moral truth. Friends reject wholly that kind of moral relativism which popularizes the idea that moral ideas are merely a function of changing culture and therefore of purely human origin. Friends hold that there is a moral order, that there are objective moral truths and that in every concrete situation there is a genuine right, however difficult it may be for finite men with their changing social patterns, to discover what it is. A corollary of this position is that entire societies may actually be wrong in what they do or in what they approve. Unless there is a real right, independent of changing cultures, it is not possible to have progress, for progress must be toward a goal. Friends are sure that progress is possible and that, in the moral reforms of which they have been pioneers, such progress has actually been demonstrated.

Existentialism. The existentialists of our day have been of radically different kinds, the greatest difference among them centering about the theistic conviction. The atheistic existentialists, particularly in France, have spread the doctrine that since all choices include evil, life is really a meaningless jumble. What is difficult to understand is why, if this is true, anyone would take the time and trouble to say so, especially in a long book. The Quaker approach to this secular thought is too obvious to merit description, but it is important to realize that this is not the only kind of existentialism that exists.

More significant for our present purpose is the consideration of those thinkers who, without failing to believe in God and life's ultimate meaning, have made us realize anew the nature of the human predicament. The degree to which they have made us realize that all human decisions are difficult, that man must pay a price for every advance and that the truth about man is always complex, they have performed a striking service. They have made it almost impossible for modern literate persons to talk glibly about the natural goodness of man and likewise impossible to talk glibly about the total depravity of man. The truth about man is that, as Pascal said, he is both little and great and both at the same time. Man's greatest sins are the sins of the spirit rather than the sins of the flesh, and paradox stands at the heart of the matter.

All this Friends are glad to accept as true. It is a gross misunderstanding of Quaker ideas to suppose that Friends have, in their doctrine of the Light Within, upheld the naïvely simple notion that man, apart from the corruptions of social organization, is naturally good. Where did the corruptions of society come from, if not from men? What Friends have maintained is the idea that men are indeed sinners, but that, in even the most depraved, there shines enough of the Light of Christ for his salvation, if only it is followed sincerely. Quakerism has always rejected both optimism and pessimism because of something better than either. Therefore, Quaker thought welcomes the existentialist analysis of the human situation, but desires to keep alive the conviction that God has not left any of His children without a witness. The favorite text of Friends in the twentieth century, as in the seventeenth, is: "This is the Light that lighteneth every man who comes into the world."

Friends can be likewise grateful to contemporary existentialism for a renewed emphasis on the old idea of the forced option. Man is a creature who must choose and the refusal to make a choice is usually itself a choice. Decision is hard for man, but it is of his very essence. We cannot wait for some ideal solution but must take the best of possible choices here and now. A thoughtful person never rejects a position merely because it has difficulties; he does not reject it unless he finds that there is a live alternative which has fewer difficulties. The recognition of this has been very good for modern Friends, helping them to be more realistic about their own choices, especially those having to do with the renunciation of war.

Behaviorism. The Behavioristic philosophy appears to be out of date but is not really so. It appears to be out of date because the term is not now much used, but the sobering fact is the degree to which the tendency persists with other words. When Professor John B. Watson first popularized the word *Behavior-*

ism, he was stressing a conception of human psychology which, theoretically, erased the distinction between men and animals. You could be very scientific, the Behaviorists suggested, in observing a rat, since, in observing him, you were not confused by his own observations or his experience. The ideal was to be equally objective about men. Psychology then would become the science of reactions to stimuli. One reaction, among others, was that of movements in the voice box, but they were not, we were told, different in character from any other physical movements of men or beasts. An integral part of this system was the elimination of all introspection, all reference to purpose, and all consideration of thinking. Purpose and thought only confused the issue because the observer could not measure them on a chart or record their intensity with any accuracy.

The absurdity of this system was so great that it fell into general disfavor, especially when people began to consider "the paradox of the thinking Behaviorist." The Behaviorist writer obviously thought that his system, which ruled out all thought, was true. But why? Was not the response of his critic as much a natural response to stimuli as his own? Thoughts, of course, can be true or false, but not actions. If we are merely beings whose actions are determined, without purpose, by external or physical forces, plus inner conditioning, both truth and goodness lose all their meaning. Like so many popular systems, Behaviorism involved inner contradictions. The notion that man was nothing but an animal could not be squared with the existence of the man who propounded it. If man was only an animal, how did he ever find that out?

Though few contemporary thinkers now call themselves Behaviorists, the idea still lives. Recently the author examined eight of the most popular textbooks in general psychology and found that only one of the eight included the word *purpose* in its index. Scrutiny showed that much of the current technique is to present an essentially mechanistic conception of human life, but without the explanation of the dogma. This may be more acceptable to the general student, but it lacks some of the honesty of the programs of Professor Watson. What is important is the contents rather than the labels.

It is clear that Quakers are bound to reject the Behavioristic concept by whatever name it uses. If man is merely one of the animals, most of what Friends have stood for is a mistake. The Quaker view is that man is indeed an animal in many ways, but that he is more. He is not merely a part of nature, because he can understand something of his place in nature and can, in striking ways, change his environment rather than merely be formed by it. In this, we believe, man is demonstrating, in spite of his stupidity and sin, his essential kinship with the Creator. Man is a creature who can assist in the creation and thus show that he is, indeed, made in God's image. Only by stressing man's qualitative differences, Friends believe, can man be brought to his rightful place in the total order. Man is small, but he knows that he is small; he is sinful, but he knows that he is a sinner. And a defect noted is one which is already partly overcome, because a creature with nothing but imperfection would never recognize it as such.

The Quaker view of the differential of man, in kind rather than merely in degree, is well supported by a great deal of careful thinking in our generation, particularly in that branch of philosophy called philosophical anthropology. The tendency to think of man in either mechanistic or biological terms, of which Behaviorism is the extreme example, has been challenged on secular grounds with marked persuasiveness. All who consider the matter are in material agreement about at least one point, that if man is an animal he is the only animal known to become a problem to himself. He is the only one who truly invents, the only one who uses tools, the only one who prays, and certainly he is the only one who philosophizes. But this is to say he is something more. Friends welcome such thinking and are quick to show that this dual nature of man, marked by his kinship with animals on the one hand and his unique interests on the other, is easily understandable if man, though in one sense a link in the biological order, is, in another sense, the creature made uniquely in the image of the Living God. The Quaker emphasis on the uniqueness of man arose, in the first place, from a deep religious experience, but it is well supported by rational thought.

As long as Quaker thought is true to its own genius it will continue to exhibit the combination of intellectual humility and of religious conviction which has marked the most creative period of Quaker life. When new systems, now unsuspected, arise—as they undoubtedly will—each must be faced with openness and without fear. Every way of thinking is necessarily based, at some point, on primitive propositions beyond which it is not possible to go. Wisdom comes by an understanding of the inevitability of this situation and by a clear understanding of what the primitive propositions are. As long as Quakers know what theirs are, they can profit from the closest contact with secular thought, both in science and in philosophy.

Quakers and the Russians
BY
ELMORE JACKSON

XIII

Quakers and the Russians

BY

ELMORE JACKSON

American Friends Service Committee Representative at the United Nations, lecturer in International Relations at Haverford College, author: *Meeting of Minds—A Way to Peace Through Mediation.*

THE SEVEN British Quakers who visited Moscow in July, 1951, characterized their approach to the Soviet authorities and people as follows:

We bore witness to our belief in God and His purpose in the world, to the eternal values which we believe to be His attributes and which have been shown most clearly in the life, the teaching and the death of Jesus Christ. We spoke to them of love, truth, sincerity, generosity; of freedom; of the value of the individual, however afflicted, mistaken or depraved; of Christianity as a way of life. Subsequently and as way opened we sought to make this message the foundation of our contribution to the many discussions we were privileged to have.

While the language differs, the essential religious approach was not unlike that which George Fox made in 1656, about 300 years earlier when he wrote to the Emperor Alexis I, beginning his communication with the words, "Friend, the Most High rules in the kingdoms of men."

This same religious note in Quaker approach to the Russians finds expression in the opening sentences in the Foreword of the small book published in 1949 under the title *The United States and the Soviet Union: Some Quaker Proposals for Peace*. This report, prepared by a "working party" of the American Friends Service Committee, begins:

> Throughout the three centuries of its history, the Society of Friends has held a testimony against war. This testimony as to the tragedy and folly of war grows out of our faith in God and our belief in the essential sacredness of human personality. It is shared by many people in our time and has been abundantly confirmed by the experiences of recent years.[1]

During the intervening years there have been many approaches to the peoples and rulers of Russia by concerned Quakers from both Great Britain and from the United States. One of the first visits was undertaken in 1818 by Stephen Grellett, a French-American Quaker who was especially interested in public education and who was concerned that nations accept arbitration as a means of settling their disputes. He was accompanied by William Allen, an English Quaker chemist. These two men had met the Czar, Alexander I, four years earlier in London and they renewed acquaintance on arrival in St. Petersburg. They explained that they came out of "a sense of religious duty laid upon us by the Great Parent of the human family." They traveled widely throughout European Russia, visiting public institutions, schools, hospitals, and prisons. While they met many who held that "learning, being an instrument of power, should be kept from the poor lest they make bad use of it," they were able to suggest certain reforms in the prison and educational systems which were carried into effect on a limited basis.

The next visit of note occurred in 1854 when the Meeting for Sufferings, the Executive Body of London Yearly Meeting, freed Joseph Sturge and two British Quaker companions to visit Czar Nicholas I, in the hopes of preventing the Crimean

---

[1] American Friends Service Committee, *The United States and the Soviet Union: Some Quaker Proposals for Peace* (New Haven: Yale University Press, 1949).

War.[2] The mission had been strongly supported by John Bright, the prominent Quaker member of parliament. In their representations to the Czar, Joseph Sturge and his companions stressed the moral and religious aspects of the problem and suggested that in a war the greatest sufferers would probably not be those who had caused the war, but innocent persons. While the mission did not succeed and war between Russia and England broke out shortly thereafter, the representations made were part of the efforts of the leading British Quakers of the time to do all within their power, both in England and in Russia, to get changes in governmental policies which might have averted the threatening disaster. John Bright had taken an especially active part in these efforts in England.

Throughout the nineteenth century the Russian government and the Orthodox Church carried on intermittent persecution of a number of the smaller religious groups. Stephen Grellet and William Allen had visited the Doukhobors, the Mennonites and the Molokans on their trip in 1818-1819. In 1892 Joseph J. Neave and John Bellows, two British Quakers, went to Russia to investigate the condition of these religious groups. During their visit they came into contact with Tolstoi and a warm friendship developed which lasted for many years. The visit aroused a great deal of interest in British and American Quaker circles, and in 1898 permission was obtained from the Russian government for the Doukhobors to leave Russia and move to Canada. While the visit of the two Friends had its humanitarian aspect, both Joseph Neave and John Bellows considered their journey to be essentially a religious mission undertaken under what Friends refer to as "religious concern."

Contact with Russian Religious Groups. While there was no direct organizational relationship between the Quakers and the organized religious groups in the Soviet Union, there has been a great deal of contact over the years with the Mennonites, Molokans, and Doukhobors. There have been certain common bonds in custom and belief. Like the Quakers they were opposed to war and, as in a number of the English-speaking countries, arrangements had been made by which their young men

---

[2] For a more complete account of Quaker journeys to Russia in the nineteenth century, see Anne Brinton's "Toward Undiscovered Ends," a Pendle Hill pamphlet published in November, 1951.

were exempted from military service. The continuation of such arrangements under the Soviet regime for certain similar groups was confirmed in a conversation between American Quakers and a Soviet official in 1946. Little is known, however, as to the extent to which such exemption arrangements have recently been used. Close contact with these religious groups has continued following their emigration to the North American continent.

Quaker religious contacts in Russia have not been confined, however, to the so-called pacifist sects. All of the visiting Quakers have had contact with the Orthodox Church leaders and, on occasion, with other church groups. One such group was the Old Believers Sect. Like the Quakers, this group had no paid ministers. They met in a simple building set aside for religious purposes or in the home of one of the members. Their meetings were conducted partially on the basis of silence. The sect maintained a strict testimony against smoking and drinking. At the time that American Quakers were negotiating with Soviet officials in 1948 over the possibility of relief work in the Ukraine and Byelorussia, one of the officials with whom contact was made proved to be a man who had grown up as a member of the Old Believers Sect. He said that because of his strict upbringing he still neither smoked nor took alcoholic beverages.

The British Quaker mission in their visit in 1951 found that most of these small sects had been drawn into an organization called the Baptist Union. Its name was taken from the fact that the Baptists were the largest religious body in the Union. It was thus in a Baptist Church, in which over 1800 people were worshiping, that Leslie Metcalf, the Chairman of the British Quaker mission to Russia, delivered the message of good-will from British Quakers and spoke of the Quaker hope that a way would be found to overcome the barriers which now separate the peoples of the "East" and "West." Talks were also held with the Archbishop and the Metropolitan of the Russian Orthodox Church in which the desire of the Western churches for closer contact with their religious brethren in the Soviet Union was stressed. The Russian church leaders were urged by members of the Quaker mission to avail themselves of the overtures which had been made in this respect by the World Council of Churches.

An Emphasis on Deeds. While Quakers have sought, as occasion offered, to speak frankly of their own religious beliefs with the hope that something said would "speak to the condition" of those they met, in dealing both with nineteenth century and twentieth century Russia, as in all other approaches, they have endeavored to retain a balance between a statement of their convictions and the demonstration of these in practice. Contacts between Quakers and Russians will always be very much in debt to Daniel Wheeler, a British Quaker seed merchant who went out to Russia in 1818, at the invitation of Czar Alexander I, and developed a successful agricultural project on a former wet and swampy area near St. Petersburg. With the help of large numbers of ex-soldiers, drainage ditches were dug, land was brought into cultivation, and eventually a model village was developed. Daniel Wheeler's home was of great help and comfort to Quaker travelers to Russia between the years of 1818 and 1832. During a period in which he was away from Russia, his wife and youngest daughter died. They are buried near the project in a plot of ground given to the Society of Friends by the Czar.

The second effort by British Quakers to be of direct rehabilitation assistance to Russian citizens occurred in 1856, after the British fleet had wantonly destroyed a number of Finnish villages included at that time within the borders of Russia. The English fleet, unable to contact the Russian fleet, had vented its anger by bombarding the villages with great loss of life and property. Joseph Sturge, who had led the mission to Moscow in the effort to avert the Crimean War, visited the area and following his report back to British Friends, relief supplies were sent.

Two British Friends visited Russia in 1891 to investigate reports of famine, but the next substantial service program entered into by Quakers was in 1916. Following an exploratory visit by four English Friends, a unit of thirty members was sent out to work in refugee and famine areas. The unit was joined in 1917 by six American Quaker women who entered Russia by way of Vladivostok. They worked until 1918 when the unit as a whole withdrew by way of Siberia.

Various efforts were made by Quakers to re-establish relief work in Russia between 1918 and 1920, but it was not until the latter year that the work was reopened and as a result both British and American Quaker teams were sent in. The American units received supplies from the American Relief Administration. The principal work was closed out in 1924, although one English Friend remained and kept the Moscow office open until 1931. The funds remaining at the end of the active field relief program were made available for the equipping of a children's clinic in Moscow.

An interesting sidelight on this post-World War I Quaker relief experience is that Alexander S. Panyushkin, who has been until recently the Soviet ambassador in Washington, was fed by the Quakers at that time and considers that they saved his life in a famine situation.

Growing out of very much the same sense of deep personal concern as that shown by Daniel Wheeler, a Baltimore Quaker and his family went to the Soviet Union in 1936 to work in connection with the anti-malarial program. Harry and Rebecca Timbers took their two children with them, and with the approval of the Moscow authorities, located in a remote forest village near the Volga. The expectations with which they entered their work and the realistic approach to its hardships are symbolized in the title of the book which Rebecca Timbers later wrote as a history of their experience, *We Didn't Ask Utopia*. Harry Timbers was stricken with typhus and died in 1937, in the midst of his active work in the village. It may be worth noting that in 1948, one of the Soviet officials with whom discussions were held in connection with the Quaker gift of streptomycin to the Russian Red Cross, had grown up in the same district of Russia in which Harry Timbers had worked and in which he had died. This official borrowed a copy of *We Didn't Ask Utopia*, saying that he wished to circulate it among a number of his Soviet colleagues. It was then to be returned. It has not been returned. One wonders if it is still circulating.

The latest Quaker offers of service occurred in 1947 and 1948.

During the spring and summer of 1947 the American Friends Service Committee had been exploring the possibilities of some relief service either in the Ukraine or in Byelorussia, following upon UNRRA's withdrawal from these areas. This possibility had been suggested by several UNRRA officials who felt that while their large program should come to a close, there were several projects in which they had been engaged which might with benefit continue for a short time to receive outside funds and be given oversight by the Service Committee. While these negotiations which would have involved the sending in of personnel were not successful, they did prepare the way for the American Friends Service Committee to make a gift of streptomycin to the Russian Red Cross in July, 1948. Each of the 4000 five-gram vials in the gift bore a label printed in the Russian language and saying: *This streptomycin is a testimony of goodwill and friendship from the American Friends Service Committee to be used to promote the health of the people of the U.S.S.R.* Three months later a message of thanks was received by cable from the Russian Red Cross. It read as follows: *The Executive Committee of the Red Cross of the U.S.S.R. is thankful to you for the streptomycin sent by you, which was distributed among children in tuberculosis hospitals and sanatoria of the U.S.S.R.* A few days later, a letter was received from the General Secretary of the Russian Red Cross giving a full insurance report. The report indicated that with the exception of a few vials which had been broken in shipment, the goodwill gift had reached its destination safely. Coming as it did, at a time when the relations between the Soviet and United States governments had been steadily growing worse, the gift met with a remarkably approving response from the American press. The response suggested that Americans of many faiths still warmly approved efforts to keep open the channels between the American and the Russian people.

It is thus, for nearly 300 years, that Quakers have sought to emphasize, in their contact with the people of Russia, that the people of both countries are members of one human family.

Some Basic Truths as Quakers See Them. What are the essential truths, as the Society of Friends sees them, which are of first importance in any present contact with the Soviet leaders and the Soviet people!

Friends have never been a group to separate out one item among their religious, social, and political beliefs and to hold it supreme over all the rest. The seven British Quakers who visited Russia in 1951 spoke of their belief in "Christianity as a way of life." There are nevertheless several points of special concern to Quakers in present-day contact with the Soviet leaders and the Soviet people?

First among these is the fact that the Quaker and Communist faiths are far apart in their interpretation of the fundamental nature of the world in which we live. The Quaker believes that there is a creating God and that that same God is still at work in the world. He believes it is possible for each individual to come into a very personal relationship with these basic spiritual forces in the universe; and that without such a relationship life is incomplete. To attempt to reform society and to lift mankind to a new level of social relationships without reference to this third dimension is to overlook the most important fact about the universe—its spiritual nature.

The coming of the atomic age has not made the Quaker faith seem less relevant to the problems which are now thrust upon us. A philosophy of economic determinism can make no enduring claim on an age in which such vast scientific power lies at the disposal of the human will. And the recent tendency of science to become subordinated to the competition between two rival political blocs can hardly continue to give comfort to those who have until now found their spiritual solace in a reverence for science. This is a time when the human heart is looking for deeper moorings and the Russian people, like other peoples, can hardly be immune from that yearning.

The English Quakers who visited Moscow came into touch with several groups of Christians in the Soviet Union. While they reported back to their sponsoring body in Great Britain that some freedom of religious observance existed in Russia, they suggested that this freedom had been secured at the cost of any independent judgment as far as the external or internal political aims of the Soviet Union were concerned. They suggested, nevertheless, that the basic religious instincts of the Russian people seemed to them to continue to a degree "which may well by their persistence confound those who look to the complete secularization of the Soviet Union." It is perhaps not without significance that in a number of recent conversations between religiously concerned Quakers and spokesmen for the Soviet Union, increasing interest has been shown in the religious and philosophical basis of Quaker social and political thought.

It would be as mistaken to assume that Quakerism could have an easy impress on modern Russia as it would have been for nineteenth century British Quakers to have assumed that the attendance of Czar Alexander I at Quaker Meetings on two occasions would have had a substantial effect on his life and practice. It is interesting, nevertheless, that Stephen Grellett and William Allen found that Robert Barclay's *Apology* (the best philosophical interpretation of the Quaker faith) was being used by one section of the Russian Orthodox Church. It is also not without some significance that Princess Metchersky had been asked by the Emperor Alexander I to translate into the Russian language William Penn's essay *No Cross, No Crown*. William Penn's conclusion "that wealth is an enemy to government and magistrates, for it tends to corruption; and the great reason why some have too little and so are forced to drudge like slaves to feed their families and keep their chin above water, is because the rich hold hard, to be richer and covet more" could hardly have been a welcome sentiment to the Russian nobility of the day. William Penn's comments are possibly still worthy of note by those who have little or no fear of the dangers inherent in the growth of the modern bureaucratic state.

One could hope that the most famous sentence of *No Cross, No Crown* might in modern Russian eyes come to be understood as characterizing at least a part of western Christendom: "True Godliness does not turn men out of the world, but enables them to live better in it, and excites their endeavors to mend it." Had this truth been a basic tenet of the Russian Orthodox Church, or in fact of western Christendom, the whole course of modern history would have been very different.

The Quaker and Communist faiths are poles apart in their belief as to the relationship of ends and means. To the Quaker each individual is sacred. Each possesses a "light within" which has the possibility of being further enkindled by a Divine light. At the opposite pole stand the forced labor camps in the Soviet Union. The existence of these camps has already severely disturbed the relationships between Russia and western countries. If one were a political optimist, one might suggest that the Soviet state might find it to its economic and moral advantage eventually to abolish the camps rather than continue to suffer the moral opprobrium which results from their continuance. But one can surmise that the camps are not likely to be abandoned quickly, for they are part of a governmental system which draws heavily on oppressive practices of the Russian past.

Thomas Shillitoe, an English Quaker who visited Russia in 1824, labored with the Czar over "the bondage of the peasants and the punishment by flogging." It was only in his second interview that he felt free to bring these questions up. He recognized they were "tender subjects for me to meddle with."

It was difficult then as now to know how to move effectively in encouraging the abandonment of practices so intimately a part of a general system of government. But it is the Christian faith that morality knows no national boundaries. We are concerned with situations of discrimination and injustice in our own country. We cannot fail to be concerned with oppressive practices in others.

Quakers believe that war is morally wrong. The Society of Friends, as its leader stated in 1660, "utterly denies all outward wars and strife and fightings with carnal weapons for any end or under any pretense whatever. This is our testimony to the whole world. . . ." The authors of *The United States and the Soviet Union*, after quoting this early Quaker statement, went on to say: "To this timeless religious and moral judgment we adhere. We believe, however, that war has now become so destructive that its folly is overwhelmingly evident to ever larger numbers of people; there are many reasons in addition to purely religious and moral ones, for questioning the validity of attempts to seek security by military means."

Great doors usually swing on more than one hinge. Shutting the door on war as a means of settling international disputes is not likely to come about by consideration only of its ethical and moral aspects. While, for the Society of Friends, these will remain the supremely important considerations, modern war has become so outmoded as a means of settling international disputes that the Soviet leaders can hardly fail to see the folly of attempting to make use of it under present conditions. Communist leaders transformed the nineteenth century conception of war as an instrument of national policy into a theory of war as an instrument of class revolution. Quakers deny equally the validity of both. While it seems unlikely that Soviet theory will make any abrupt change, it is perhaps not too much to hope that out of a continuous and careful appraisal of the consequences of modern war, Soviet practice might gradually alter to the point at which new attention is given, both in the Soviet Union and in the countries of the "West," to other means of resolving international disputes.

The Alternatives to Violence. William Penn and John Bellers both included Russia in their general plans for the peace of Europe. Joseph Sturge, undeterred by his failure along with John Bright to avert the Crimean War, drew up a suggested provision which would have bound the signers of the Treaty of Paris, which ended that war, to submit their disputes to arbitration. To the surprise of many of his associates, a revised provision was finally adopted unanimously urging the signatories to undertake arbitration before resorting to arms.

The attention given *The United States and the Soviet Union* and the more recent pamphlet published by the American Friends Service Committee entitled "Steps to Peace," indicates that ideas put forward by Quakers as to the way in which international relations can be brought into a more ordered form continue to be of some interest on both sides of the iron curtain. Sixty-five thousand copies of the former were distributed in the United States and it was translated into four different languages. The distribution of the latter went to ninety-five thousand copies in the United States, with a special edition in England. Both studies were well read east of Berlin.

The spectacularly rapid growth in international communications has brought the world into a disconcertingly small compass. The administrative problem appears now to be not so much the question of whether we shall have more ordering of our economic and political life through international agencies but the question of the form which the growth in international institutions will take. Will the development be on a universal basis, extending the present work of the United Nations, or will the emphasis be on the growth of regional institutions? Are NATO and the Cominform only the first response to the new power rivalry in the world or will they gradually take over the stage, forcing the rest of the world either to take sides or, in attempted self-defense, to create independent regional groupings of their own?

On this question we already are midstream in the decisive decade. Surely it is not too much to hope that American statesmanship will grasp the great new political truth of our time—that the future of democracy and freedom in the United States is now intimately tied with the struggle for political freedom and for economic and social justice in every country. To flag in our efforts to create universal instruments of government is to take ourselves out of the race and to misunderstand the nature of the forces which have made European dominance already a thing of the past.

From the time of William Penn, Friends have tended to favor a universal approach to the organization of peace. They were active in support of and in the work of the League of Nations. In *The United States and the Soviet Union* the authors suggest that "a main purpose of United States policy should be to strengthen and develop the United Nations." Nations were urged voluntarily to refer disputes to a two-thirds vote of the most relevant United Nations organ. The Permanent Members of the Security Council were urged to consider again an agreement limiting the use of the veto, and specifically exempting from its purview the admission of new Members to the United Nations. Proposals along these lines were further developed in "Steps to Peace."

While many Friends continue to be interested in United Nations Charter revision and probably the great majority would urge the progressive acceptance of arbitration and judicial settlement as a means of settling international disputes, increasing attention has been given of late to the possibilities of developing the mediation functions of the United Nations. In this critical period the political work of the United Nations would appear to stand or fall on the success of the Organization in the peaceful settlement of disputes. It is for this reason that recent Quaker work at the United Nations has come to center more and more around the ways in which the mediatory functions of the Organization could be developed to make maximum use of previous successful mediation experience, both in the United Nations and in other fields of conflict settlement. The recently published *Meeting of Minds* [3] is one of the first of the Quaker studies devoted exclusively to this concern.

Diminishing the Incentives to Conflict. While many of the world's political problems must be taken up and dealt with in a forthright fashion in the initial context in which they are presented, it is sometimes necessary to let some of these political problems rest while efforts are made to change the basic circumstances in which they appear. Thus while Count Bernadotte and Ralph Bunche were able to negotiate a truce between the Jewish and Arab interests in Palestine, it is unlikely that a political peace will be achieved by the United Nations until the economic problems which presently aggravate the Middle-Eastern situation are somewhat eased. In some measure this may be the situation with regard to the political problems which now so deeply divide "East" and "West."

It was perhaps inevitable that political systems would grow up in the great land masses of North America and of Asia which would at some stage in the world's development face each other in bitter rivalry. This does not mean, however, that large-scale military conflict between them is in any sense inevitable. Both the United States and the Soviet Union have a tremendous

[3] Elmore Jackson, *Meeting of Minds* (New York: McGraw-Hill Book Company, Inc., 1952).

stake in avoiding the catastrophic and the entirely unparalleled destruction which war would bring to each nation.

Soviet attitudes and policies are a reflection of their outlook on the modern world. Believing that their philosophy is destined to triumph, they see in the awakening of primitive peoples and the revolt against oppressive colonial practices a vindication of their theories and an opportunity for communist advancement. They see a world in which the Europeans and Americans have set up color bars and have attempted to maintain economic and social privileges. It would be too much to suppose that they would fail to make full use of these facts in their power struggle with the "West."

The "Point IV liberals" of the "West" talk a bit glibly about the ease with which their countries can put in order their relations with the less developed countries to forestall a turn to the tenets of communism. A reconstruction of relationships will, in fact, be an appallingly difficult task—for our hostages to the status quo are very substantial. As the British have found in giving India its freedom and as the Dutch have similarly found in relation to Indonesia, the giving of political freedom cuts deeply into the standard of living of the metropolitan power.

The extent to which the United States has come under a new sense of responsibility is illustrated by the short space of four years between the derision which characterized the first suggestions for non-European economic aid as "a quart of milk for every Hottentot" and the range of the economic provisions of the last multi-billion dollar Mutual Security Bill passed by the Congress. The first impromptu response to the enlarged responsibility of the United States has been economic aid and enormous funds for military purposes. The more realistic approach must now come: (1) a moral leadership which puts the United States' shoulder behind the wheel of economic and social progress in these less developed areas, and (2) new approaches to disarmament, which if successful could release great new funds for international economic development. In the United States' inspired consideration of land reform programs in the United Nations Economic and Social Council, in the United States' acquiescence in the United Nations study of an International Development Authority and in the renewed, even if still halting, reconsideration of disarmament one sees the beginning of such leadership.

The great disparity which still exists, however, between the small amounts set aside for economic aid and the vastly greater sums appropriated for military purposes in these areas suggests that the Congress has not yet come to understand the problems of underdeveloped peoples. Economic aid can help them meet their needs in internal development but equally fundamental is their need to be brought into a sense of political equality and into cultural fellowship with the more highly developed countries of the "West." The fact that only New Zealand and Australia were prepared to join the United States in a Pacific Defense Council (making it an all Anglo-Saxon team) suggests that the United States hasn't yet discovered the key to Asia.

A Growing Sense of Responsibility. While the Society of Friends has acquired a certain reputation for the impartial distribution of relief, and many of its 150,000 members have been active in a wide variety of reform movements, this chapter suggests a number of the instances in which members of the Society have carried their concerns to those in positions of authority and power, in Russia, and their own countries.

These representations have frequently dealt with the most complex problems of international life. They have never been made out of a belief that Quakers possessed a special key which could unlock these situations. They have grown out of a deep religious and moral concern over particular developments, and such appropriateness as the representations have achieved has been related to this and to the special circumstances in which Friends found themselves.

It is not because Friends feel that in some special way they have unique insight into present-day international problems that they have taken a special interest in the work of the United Nations both in Geneva and in New York and have, during the past three sessions of the General Assembly, brought together international Quaker teams to observe and confer with delegates, as appropriate, on matters of special concern to Friends.

It is just that the decisions concerning war and peace are now so dreadfully important and, to use a non-Quaker phrase, the "stakes" are now so terribly high. Out of this sustained work there has come, I believe, a greater understanding on the part of Friends of the complexities which the world's statesmen face. At the same time Friends may have made some small contribution in helping keep the channels of communication open between those who make high policy and some of those millions who are so soon affected by it.

If there should be continuing opportunities for Quakers to present and discuss their concerns with those who hold high office in Russia and in the western world, it would scarcely be in accord with past history for them to be timid about making use of such openings. It would seem likely that Quakers in the future, as in the past, will in any such discussions be especially concerned with support for the United Nations and its Specialized Agencies, with the need for more adequate programs of economic development, with the development of an effective plan for disarmament, and with the mutually aggravating effects, in the "East-West" conflict, of policies of internal subversion.

The world of the next decade is hardly likely to be a place where the fainthearted will feel at home. Once we have fully grasped the revolutionary character of the world in which we live, we will, I believe, realize three minimal prerequisites for effective leadership in matters related to the "East-West" conflict.

1. It is essential, in both the religious and political fields, that we know what we believe. The approach to those who differ with us may be one of "I am myself persuaded, I suggest you see for yourself," but the future will call for greater clarity in both religious and political beliefs.

2. There must be a new unity between belief and practice. Modern communication leaves few aspects of human weakness undisclosed. We must make a more imaginative and sustained effort to live out what we believe.

3. We must be more forthright in stating the kind of world we want; not just the kind of world we would like for ourselves

as Americans; not even just the kind of world we want for all those outside the communist-dominated areas; but the kind of world we want for all, including the people of Russia. Only then can we begin to remove the miasma of fear and only then will we find that the minds of men have been uplifted.

Epilogue
BY
CLARENCE E. PICKETT

Epilogue

BY

CLARENCE E. PICKETT

Honorary Secretary of the American Friends Service Committee; served twenty years as Executive Secretary of the Committee.

SPEAKERS IN A Quaker meeting for worship are supposed to give vocal utterance "when the spirit moves." But anyone who has long attended such meetings soon realizes that what is being said, if it is effective, is in the vernacular of today, with the stamp of today's world on it. It is not a strange language tuned to the climate of three centuries ago when the Society of Friends was born. At its best, present-day ministry has an unmistakable divine urge in it. But phrases and context are thoroughly of today. If we discuss war, it is not in the context of bows and arrows, but of atomic bombs. If we have a concern about economics, its context is not the barter economy of mid-eighteenth century, but it presupposes a modern industrial society. This is one reason why it is necessary repeatedly to restate the position of Friends with regard to varying phases of life. "Through the ages one unceasing purpose runs." One finds throughout the history of Quakerism one continuous understanding of the nature of God and of human beings and their relations to each other. But as the practices of our external life change with the changing world, we must rethink these abiding convictions and their application to life about us. In 1922, British Quakers published a volume called *Christian Life, Faith, and Thought in the Society of Friends.* This consists of a collection of individual statements and group pronouncements on various phases of religious and secular life. It shows the altered methods that have been used in applying a continuing experience with Truth to changing patterns of daily life. It is one of our most valuable documents.

The volume here published under the title *The Quaker Approach* is another effort in that tradition of restatement. The application of those principles are rethought in the light of changed customs and practices. Belief in the essential oneness of all mankind does not change. But the problems of race relations are quite different now from those that prevailed in the days of human slavery. Likewise, whoever heard of strong arguments concerning private enterprise fifty years ago? But with the revolutionary trend toward collectivism we must now rethink our practice concerning socialism, collectivism, and other forms of property control. There is intellectual turmoil in the field of philosophical thought, in education, and in the application of psychiatry to physical and mental health.

Especially the development of modern Science and its challenge on the one hand to divine revelation and on the other to the morality of its application to personal and especially international living calls for incisive thought and clear-cut conscience to help us all find how we can be both scientifically minded and divinely guided.

Especially, too, we American Friends must rethink our way as citizens of a country which has newly reached political, economic, and military power. We now take the center of the stage on one side of a great power battle. Can Friends keep their eyes on universal values? Can we view all men as children of God? Can we help to release the healing stream of divine love without being sucked into the battle for power? Here we shall need our best thought and our most courageous action.

The growing strength and penetration of government action in new forms forces us to consider not so much whether we shall "render unto Caesar the things that are Caesar's and unto God things that are God's," but to determine what things are Caesar's and what are God's. Shall we with gratitude see the problems of personal and social security taken out of the hands of Christian generosity and placed at the mercies of the state? The state taxes us heavily to support a military establishment whose existence we contend thwarts the growth of understanding among nations to which we are deeply committed. To find our way in this tangled web of state and private responsibility, our practice has to be re-explored. Here in *The Quaker Approach* are statements from Friends of various countries who have wrestled, each in his own sphere of exploration, with both the intellectual and the practical problems that our secular world presents those who try to live in the power of a religious spirit. The effort will never be concluded. It must be faced by each generation. We of today are blest by reasonably accurate records of the honest and often fruitful efforts of Friends of the past in this struggle. In so far as the Society of Friends carries any particular weight in the present day, it is as our generation tries to bring together profession and practice. We freely recognize that this struggle is not peculiar to Quakers. In many respects it is the common struggle at least of all Christians. But we who are members of the Society of Friends have little to fall back on except our experience with Truth. We cannot resort to ritual or creed or ecclesiastical decisions for guidance. We must find our way by seeing the hand of God at work in the weaving of the fabric of daily life. We dare to hope that the reading of these records of current thought may add to the wisdom and enrich the spiritual heritage of all who seek to bring intellectual consistency and spiritual power into current life.

This volume goes forth not as a final word but as guide and stimulant to a seeking people today. It will realize its maximum purpose if readers find firm ground on which to stand as they wrestle with changing events about them.

GEORGE ALLEN & UNWIN LTD
London: 40 Museum Street, W.C.1

Auckland: Haddon Hall, City Road
Sydney, N.S.W.: Bradbury House, 55 York Street
Cape Town: 58-60 Long Street
Bombay: 15 Graham Road, Ballard Estate, Bombay 1
Calcutta: 17 Chittaranjan Avenue, Calcutta 13
New Delhi: Munshi Niketan, Kamla Market, Ajmeri Gate, New Delhi 1
Karachi: Haroon Chambers, South Napier Road, Karachi 2
Toronto: 91 Wellington Street West
Sao Paulo: Avenida 9 de Julho 1138-Ap. 51

APR 1 6 1989